Jesus
The Healer

E.W.KENYON
Author
(1867-1948)

Thirty-Second Printing

CONTENTS

FIRST WORDS

HIS little book with its mighty message comes from the very heart of the Master to you. If you have been defeated in life's fight, if you have failed to get into the program of success, this little book will show you how to win.

If you are sick, there is healing for you.

If you are weak, it will give you strength.

If you are discouraged, it will put the spirit of a conqueror into you.

Be honest with it. Don't read it with your mind full of preconceived notions.

Go to it fairly, honestly, and let it put you over the mountain that stands between you and Victory.

Chapter I

THE TWO KINDS OF KNOWLEDGE

NE of the recent discoveries in our spiritual laboratory has been that there are two kinds of knowledge.

The knowledge that our schools, colleges, and universities teach has come to us through the Five Senses.

It is safe to say that there is no knowledge of Chemistry, Biology, Metallurgy, or Mechanics, or any other field of research, but that which has come to us through the Five Senses --- Seeing, Tasting, Hearing, Smelling, and Feeling.

Our bodies have really been the laboratory in which the research work has steadily gone on through the ages.

That knowledge is limited. It cannot find the human spirit.

It cannot discover how the mind functions in the physical brain.

It cannot find God, nor discover the origin of Matter, of Life, of Force, or of Creation.

All that it can discover are things it can See, Hear, Taste, Smell, or Feel.

We call it, "Sense Knowledge."

Then there is another kind of knowledge that has come to us through the Revelation called the Bible.

This is Revelation Knowledge.

It brings us in contact with the Creator.

It explains the "Why" of Creation, the Reason for Man, the Nature of Man, and the ultimate goal of Man.

It deals with things that the Senses cannot discover or know without assistance from this Revelation Knowledge.

The unhappy fact is that Sense Knowledge has gained the supremacy in the Church.

The Church is a spiritual organization, a spiritual body, to be governed through the spirit instead of through the senses.

When Sense Knowledge gained the ascendancy in the Church and the fountain of the Church, the theological school, the Church ceased to be a spiritual body and simply became a body of men governed by Sense Knowledge.

You can see why Sense Knowledge, which cannot understand spiritual things, will deny miracles, will deny answers to prayer, and will deny the deity of Jesus, discrediting His Resurrection and miracles.

It is to be expected that Sense Knowledge will deny the miraculous, because it cannot explain it or understand it.

The chief quest of Sense Knowledge has been for reality. Man's spirit craves it.

Reality cannot be found by the Senses. It is only discovered by the spirit. *seated w/ christ in 3rd Heaven*

Sense Knowledge has sent forth men called Philosophers, searchers after Reality.

It is a profound fact, worthy of every man's consideration, that the man who really knows Jesus Christ, who has received Eternal Life, never turns to Philosophy.

If he has been a Philosopher, he gives it up because he has arrived at reality in Christ.

Jesus said, "I am the way, the reality, and the life." Jesus, then, is the answer to all true Philosophy.

If you wish to study this subject more fully, send for our little book, "The Two Kinds of Knowledge."

Chapter II

GOD IS A FAITH GOD

I NEVER knew the "Why'" of faith until I read Hebrews 11:3. "By faith we understand that the worlds have been framed (or created) by the word of God, so that what is seen hath not been made out of things which do appear."

Like a flash I grasped the secret of Genesis 1. "In the beginning God created."

How did He create? By the Word of Faith. *Able to call forth and manifest & healing*

He said, "Let there be." He created with words. *with the word becoming flesh*

Jesus knew the secret of words. He healed the sick with words. He raised the dead with words. He stilled the sea with, "Peace be still."

Peter healed the sick by using the Name of Jesus. Paul cast out demons by saying, "In the Name of Jesus Christ, come out."

They used words that were born of faith. They were Faith's words.

We become the sons of God, partakers of His very nature, by acting on words.

We become faith men and women, we use faith words, and we produce faith results.

Faith in My Faith

The first time those words came to me they startled me. I began to examine myself and ask the question, "Why is it that people haven't faith in their own faith?" They have faith in my faith.

I receive letters from many far away countries asking for prayer.

Why? Because the people who ask for prayer haven't confidence in their own faith.

For some reason they do not believe in themselves. They do not believe in what Christ has wrought for them, or what they are in Christ.

The reason for their unbelief is that they do not know what they are in Christ. They have a feeling that they are not good enough, that their faith is not strong enough.

They are acquainted with all of their own failings and weaknesses.

They accept every condemnation from the pulpit. They are willing always to believe anything against themselves, their unworthiness, their unfitness, their weakness, their lack of faith.

Here are some facts:
The Father has no favorites. Every person born into His Family has the same Redemption.

He has been redeemed out of the hand of his enemy. Satan was conquered for him personally.

He can say, "He was delivered up on the account of my trespasses and He was raised for my justification."

He can confidently say, "Who delivered me out of the authority of darkness, and translated me into the kingdom of the Son of His love. In whom I have my redemption, the remission of my trespasses."

It is a personal, an absolute Redemption from the dominion of the Adversary.

Christi Was Your Substitute

When Jesus put Satan to naught and stripped him of his authority, it was you, in Christ, who did that work. Christ acted in your stead; He did it for you.

You can say, "In Christ, I conquered Satan. I stripped him of his authority, and when Jesus arose from the dead, I arose with Him."

You can confidently say, "But God being rich in mercy with His great love wherewith He loved me, even when I was dead through my trespasses and sins, made me alive together with Christ (By grace have I been saved, or healed) and raised me up with Him, and made me to sit with Him in the heavenlies in Christ."

It is when you take your place and begin to assume your rights and privileges that God begins to respond to you. You have the same Eternal Life that Jesus had.

"He that hath the Son hath the life." You have the Son; you have the Life.

Now you may say, "I have taken Jesus Christ as my Savior. I have confessed Him as my Lord. God has given to me Eternal Life, His own nature. I am now a new creation, created in Christ Jesus, and I have God's ability to perform the good works that were afore prepared that I should walk in them.

"I have God's ability because I have God's nature. I have the same great, mighty Spirit who raised Jesus from the dead dwelling in me.

"Greater is he that is in me, than he that is in the world."

You Are His Righteousness

You have the same Righteousness as Jesus. "Him who knew no

sin, God made to be sin on your behalf; that you might become the Righteousness of God in Him." (2 Cor. 5:21.)

You can say, "I have become the Righteousness of God in Him.

"There is therefore now no condemnation to me, because I am in Christ Jesus."

That Righteousness gives you the privilege of standing in the Father's presence as though you had never committed sin.

You have His nature. You are His very own child. He is your Father.

You can say, "He has declared me Righteous. He has made me Righteous. I am the Righteousness of God in Christ."

As a son you have the legal right to use the Name of Jesus.

No one has a better right to the use of the Name of Jesus than you.

All Authority Is In That Name

Now you say with me, "Jesus declares that whatever I ask in His Name, He will give it to me; fearlessly I take my place. I lay my hands upon that loved one who is sick and say, 'In the Name of Jesus, Disease, leave this body; Demon, leave this body and go off into the abyss where you belong. Don't you ever touch this loved one again.'

"Christ said to me that they who believe should lay hands on the sick, and they should recover. 'In my name they shall cast out demons.' He said this to me. I accept it at its face value and I act upon it because He said it to me."

Chapter III

THE FATHER HAS NO FAVORITES

I was a great comfort to my heart when I realized that the Father has no favorites, that all the children have their own place in His heart.

He loves each one of them even as He loves the Lord Jesus.

Jesus said, "That the world may know, that thou lovedst them even as thou lovedst me."

We all have the same Redemption.

The work that He wrought in Christ absolutely destroyed the power of the enemy, and now redeems every person who will accept Christ as Savior and confess Him as Lord.

That Redemption is from the works of the adversary and from his dominion over our lives.

Everyone has the same Righteousness. No one has a better Righteousness, or more Righteousness.

Righteousness comes through the New Creation. When we are Born Again, we receive the life and nature of God, the Father.

His nature makes us Righteous. No one has more of it than another.

All who receive His nature have come into the Family and are recognized as the sons and daughters of the great Father-God.

Everyone has the same rights in the Family.

Each one may have a different gift, but the gift does not make him any dearer to the heart of the Father.

Everyone has the same love nature, the same great Holy Spirit who raised Jesus from the dead.

Each one has a right to the same kind of fellowship with the Father.

Each one has a right to the use of the Name of Jesus.

Each one has a right to the authority invested in that Name to deliver people from the dominion of Satan, to heal the sick, and to cast out demons.

The Father has no favorites.

The closer your fellowship is with the Father, the sweeter and richer your life will be.

Chapter IV

THE LIVING WORD

THE problem of healing is a problem of the integrity of the Word. Many have never recognized it, but the Word is the healer today.

God, in Christ, wrought a perfect Redemption. In that Redemption there is perfect healing for every believer; but because of lack of knowledge of the Word, Christians everywhere are sick.

Psalm 107:20 perfectly illustrates this. "He sent His Word and healed them."

John 1:1, "In the beginning was the Word, and the Word was with God, and the Word was God."

14th verse, "And the Word became flesh, and dwelt among us (and we beheld his glory, glory as of the only begotten from the Father) full of grace and truth."

That is the Word He sent. He had sent His spoken Word through the prophets. The living Word was made flesh.

Now He unveils the life-giving Word in the Gospels and the Epistles. John 6:63; Hebrews 4:12 (Moffett's trans.).

"The words that I have spoken unto you are spirit, and are life."

"For the Logos of God is a living thing, active and more cutting than any sword with double edge, penetrating to the very division of soul and spirit, joint and marrow – scrutinizing the very thoughts and conceptions of the heart."

The Word becomes a living thing only as we act upon it.

The Word is God speaking. It is always a present-tense fact. You might say that the Word is always now, just as God is always now.

The Word is a part of God, Himself. God and His Word are one, just as you and your word are one.

The Word is the will of the Father, just as Jesus, the Word made flesh, was the will of the Father during His earthly ministry.

What God says, is; what God says, will become. Had He not wanted it to be, He would not have said it.

You can depend upon His Word utterly. You have depended upon institutions and men.

Institutions may fail, individuals may die, nations may disintegrate, but God cannot deny Himself.

Behind the Word is the integrity of God. Not only is His integrity behind the Word, but His very throne is involved in His Word.

Hebrews 7:22 declares that Jesus is the surety of the New Covenant. "By so much also hath Jesus become the surety of a better covenant."

He is back of every word from Matthew to Revelation. Every word was God-breathed.

The throne upon which Jesus is seated is back of every Word

Faith, Hope, and Mental Assent

There must be a clear distinction in your mind between Believing and Mental Assent.

Believing the Word is acting on the Word.

Mental Assent is acknowledging the truthfulness of the Word, the integrity of the Word, but never acting upon it.

Mental Assent is standing outside the bakery and coveting the cake in the window. It is not possessing.

Hope is not faith. It is not Believing. Hope is always living in the future.

Faith is always now. It is not passivity. Passivity lies quietly without action, without choice, inert.

Believing is acting on the Word.

Believing the Word is not only recognizing its utter truthfulness, but it is taking it to be your very own now.

To act on His Word is to do His will and to act in His will.

He is honored by our acting on the Word.

He is dishonored by our Mentally Assenting to its truthfulness, by our hoping that it will become true sometime, and by our passivity that lies quietly rejoicing in the Word but has no part in it.

"He that believeth hath." If you believe, you have!

His Name is glorified by our acting on the Word. The Father is glorified by our acting on the Word.

Remember that His throne is back of His Word. His integrity is involved in it.

John 15:7, "If ye abide in me, and my words abide in you, ask whatsoever ye will, and it shall be done unto you. Herein is my Father glorified, that ye bear much fruit; and so shall ye be my disciples."

That is the fruit of the indwelling Word which has prompted prayers that are answered.

The Case Stated

There are two views of healing.

The most common view is that healing is not in the Redemptive work of Christ, but belongs to us if we have faith enough to claim it.

This belief holds that faith is the gift of God. If God gives you faith for your healing, you will be healed. If He does not give you faith, there is no need to struggle for your healing. Your only hope is the arm of flesh.

This view is superficial. It is the result of Sense Knowledge.

Sense Knowledge is the knowledge of natural man that is gained through the Senses. It is the kind of knowledge taught in all our technical schools and universities.

The other kind of knowledge is Revelation Knowledge. It teaches that miracles are for today.

Sense Knowledge repudiates it in a very large measure because it is above the knowledge of the Senses.

The second view of healing is that it is a part of the plan of Redemption, that disease came with the fall, and that sickness is a work of the adversary.

Because disease came with the fall, God is the natural, logical Healer.

Man cannot deal with the sin problem. He cannot make himself Righteous. He cannot rid himself of sin-consciousness.

These can only come through the finished work of Christ. God planned that when we were recreated (the recreation which comes through our receiving the nature and life of God) we would be Righteous, and partake of His Righteousness which is His very nature. This would give us the position of sons.

The New Creation is more than being baptized or confirmed. It is receiving the Life and Nature of the Father. Our spirits are recreated by receiving Eternal Life.

Isaiah 53 holds the key of Redemption. Jesus was made sin with our sins. Not only was He made sin with our sins, but He was made sick with our sicknesses.

Natural man is called Sin.

2 Corinthians 6:14-16, "Be not unequally yoked with unbelievers: for what fellowship hath righteousness and iniquity? or what communion hath light with darkness?"

The believer is called Righteousness; the unbeliever is called Iniquity.

He has not only committed sin, but he is sin.

The Believer is called Light and the unbeliever is called Darkness.

Just as the sinner is "sin," the sick man is not only sick, but he is "sickness." Sin deals with the spirit; sickness is a spiritual thing revealed in the body.

"And what concord hath Christ with Belial?" The believer is called Christ, because Christ is a part of the body. The branch is a part of the vine. It is as much a part of the vine as the vine itself.

1 Corinthians 12:12, "For as the body is one, and hath many members, and all the members of the body, being many, are one body; so also is Christ.

The man outside of Christ is called Belial. That perfectly agrees with I John 3: 10.

"In this the children of God are manifest, and the children of the devil."

When God laid our sin on Jesus, He laid us on Jesus. He laid the whole man on Jesus. He laid his sins, his weaknesses, his infirmities and diseases, his union with the adversary, on Jesus. Jesus became sin with our sin, became sick with our sickness.

Isaiah 53:10, "Yet it pleased Jehovah to bruise him; he hath put him to grief." Another translation reads, "It pleased Jehovah to crush Him with disease; He hath made Him sick."

6th verse, "All we like sheep have gone astray; we have turned everyone to his own way; and Jehovah hath laid on him the iniquity of us all."

Afflicted In Spirit

Jesus was made sick with our sicknesses. He was made sin with our sin. This was God's method of dealing with the sin problem.

He settled the sin problem.

There is no sin problem. Christ put sin away, and satisfied the claims of justice for man.

The real problem is the "sinner problem."

There is no sickness problem. There is simply a problem of the believer's coming to know his inheritance in Christ.

When John the Baptist said, John 1:29, "Behold, the Lamb of God, that taketh away the sin of the world!" he was giving public notice that this Man whom he had baptized was the Sin-Substitute, the Sickness-Substitute for the human race.

Sin and sickness come from the same source.

Satan is the author of both. I am sure that it is God's order that the believer should be as free from sickness as he is from sin. He should be as free from the fear of disease as he is from the condemnation of sin.

14

God cannot see sin in the New Creation. Neither can He see sickness in the New Creation.

James wrote, "Is any sick among you?"

There should not be any sick among you, but if there is anyone sick, this tells what he should do.

It was the plan of the Father that every believer should know what Peter tells us in 1 Peter 2:24, "Who his own self bare our sins in his body upon the tree, that we, having died unto sins, might live unto righteousness; by whose stripes ye were healed."

He wants us to know that when He laid our sins and sicknesses on Jesus and Jesus bore them away, it was to the end that sin and disease should no longer have dominion over us.

He wants us to know in the second place, that sickness and disease do not belong in the Family of God.

If there should be any sickness among us, it is because of a low state of knowledge of our rights and privileges in our Redemption. It is due to a lack of knowledge of the fact that God, by laying our diseases on Christ, has settled the disease problem in Redemption.

We should be as free from the fear of sickness as we are free from the condemnation of sin. Both are of the adversary.

At the New Birth, sins are all remitted. The sin nature is displaced by the nature of God.

Disease leaves with the sins.

So the Father can see no sickness in the New Creation. He put it all on Christ.

When we recognize the fact that our sickness was laid on Christ, and that He bore our diseases in His body on the tree, and that by His stripes we are healed, it will be the end of the dominion of disease in our lives.

But this knowledge is of no value until your heart says, "Surely He bore my diseases and my pains, and by His stripes I am healed" just as though you were the only sick person in the world.

* * * * * * * * * * *

The Word is like God – eternal. It cannot be destroyed.

He watches over it to make it good.

His Word brought man into being. Now He is building Himself into man through the Word.

The Word is part of Himself, and it is this Self that is changing the conduct of believers and bringing them into harmony with Himself.

He shares Himself with us; He gives us His nature in the New Creation. He makes Himself one with us.

We are united with Him in the New Birth.

We are to take advantage of this union. His Nature gives us new ability, new wisdom and we must take advantage of it.

His strength is ours. His life is ours.

His health is ours; His ability is ours.

Disease is Satan's work.

When you tell anyone of it, you glorify him. You ignore the fact that God laid that disease upon Jesus and that He put it away.

The Word says that you are healed. Get used to acting on the Word.

Chapter V

THE VALUE OF CONFESSION

T is necessary that there be a continual confession of our Redemption from Satan's dominion and that he no longer rules us with condemnation nor fear of disease.

We hold fast to this confession, as our confession is Satan's defeat.

We believers do not ask to be healed, because we have been healed.

We do not ask to be made Righteous, because we have been made Righteous.

We do not ask to be Redeemed, for our Redemption is an absolute fact.

In the mind of the Father, we are perfectly healed and perfectly free from sin, because He laid our diseases and our sins upon His Son.

His Son was made sin with our sins. He was made sick with our diseases.

In the mind of Christ, we are perfectly healed because He can remember when He was made sin with our sins, when He was made sick with our diseases. He remembers when He put our sin and our diseases away.

In the mind of the Holy Spirit we are absolutely free from both, for He remembers when Christ was made sin and when He was made sick. He remembers when He raised Jesus from the dead.

Christ was free from our sin and our sickness. Both had been put away before His Resurrection.

The Word declares that "By His stripes we were healed."

The whole problem is our recognition of the absolute truthfulness of that Word.

It is not good taste to ask Him to heal us, for He has already done it.

This truth came with a shock when I first saw it. He declared that we are healed; therefore we are.

The only problem now is to get in perfect harmony with His Word.

If He declares we are healed, then our part is to thank Him for the work He has already accomplished.

Renewing of the Mind

I feel I should introduce another subject for a moment. That is the renewing of our minds. It is only the Renewed mind that can grasp these truths.

Your spirit has been recreated, but not your mind. Heretofore, it has received all of its knowledge through the senses, so it must be renewed.

Romans 12:2, "And be not fashioned according to this world: but be ye transformed by the renewing of your mind, that ye may prove what is the good and acceptable and perfect will of God."

The same truth is brought out in Titus 3:5 and Ephesians 4:23 and Colossians 3:10.

"Not by works done in righteousness, which we did ourselves, but according to his mercy he saved us, through the washing of regeneration and renewing of the Holy Spirit."

"And that ye be renewed in the spirit of your mind, and put on the new man, that after God hath been created in righteousness and holiness of truth."

"And have put on the new man, that is being renewed unto knowledge after the image of him that created him."

This renewing of the mind comes through meditation and action on the Word.

As soon as one is Born Again, he should ask the Holy Spirit to come in and make His home in his body.

Luke 11:13 shows the Father's attitude in regard to it.

"How much more shall your heavenly Father give the Holy Spirit to them that ask him?"

As surely as we ask Him, so surely will the Spirit make His home in our bodies.

The renewed mind sees that all there is to be done for its healing is to praise the Father for it. It says, "My diseases were laid on Christ and He put them away. I am healed. I thank the Father that it is done."

The pain may be there. The soreness may be in evidence. These are only the testimony of the Senses.

We refuse to listen to the witness of our senses. We accept the Word of God and act upon it. As surely as God sits on the throne, He will make that Word good in us.

We do not ask for power, for He who is the power is in us.

We do not ask for wisdom, for Christ was made wisdom unto us.

We do not ask for Redemption, for He is our Redemption.

We do not ask for Sanctification, for He is made unto us Sanctification.

We do not ask for Righteousness, because He is made unto us Righteousness.

This faith life is the most beautiful thing in the world. We step out of the old Sense realm where we have lived.

We have always lived with Thomas. He said, John 20:25, "Except I shall see in his hands the print of the nails, and put my finger into the print of the nails, and put my hand into his side, I will not believe."

Jesus met him and said, "Reach hither thy finger, and see my hands; and reach hither thy hand, and put it into my side: and be not faithless, but believing."

Then Thomas cried, "My Lord and my God."

But Jesus said to him, "Because thou hast seen me, thou hast believed: blessed are they that have not seen and yet have believed."

We should not need the evidence of the senses. Let us rest on the Word.

Ephesians 1:3, "Blessed be the God and Father of our Lord Jesus Christ, who hath blessed us with every spiritual blessing in the heavenlies in Christ."

You are in the family. Everything that the Father has belongs to the children. You are one of them. You have been blessed.

Healing for the World

God meets man where he is.

Most of the healings that were performed by the apostles and the early church were among men and women who had not yet become Christians. They were heathens, or they were Jews.

Healing was God's method of advertising, God's method of revealing Himself to the natural mind.

Jesus was an intrusion into the Sense realm. The church, the New Creation, was an invasion into the Sense realm.

But today the Sense Knowledge men have invaded the church and taken it captive.

The Sense realm is the realm of the natural man, that is, the man who believes only what he can hear, taste, smell, feel, or see.

God's intrusion into that realm in the person of His Son as head of the church was a miraculous invasion.

Mark 16:16-21 gives us evidence for this.

"He that believeth and is baptized shall be saved; but he that disbelieveth shall be condemned. And these signs shall accompany them that believe."

* * * * * * * * * * *

Our confession imprisons us or sets us free.

A strong confession coupled with a corresponding action on the Word brings God on the scene.

Holding fast to one's confession when the senses contradict shows that one has become established in the Word.

A Satan-inspired confession is always dangerous.

Remember that he brought that disease, put it upon you.

Your acknowledgement of the disease is like signing for a package that the express company has left you. Satan then has the receipt for your disease. You have accepted it.

"Surely He hath borne our sickness and carried our diseases" is God's receipt for our perfect healing.

A positive confession dominates circumstances, while a vacillating confession permits circumstances to govern one.

Your confession is what God says about your disease.

A negative confession will make the disease stronger.

Then your confession heals or keeps you sick.

The confession of your lips should have your heart's full agreement.

Chapter VI

"THESE SIGNS"

AS soon as a man believed, these signs were to accompany him. "In my name shall they cast out demons; they shall speak with new tongues; they shall take up serpents, and if they drink any deadly thing, it shall in no wise hurt them; they shall lay hands on the sick, and they shall recover."

The word "believer" means "a believing one."

As soon as a man was Born Again, God planned that he should advertise the New Creation by healing sick folk in the presence of the unsaved world.

Jesus' entire ministry was a combat with the demonical forces.

The same thing is true of the church. All disease, all sickness, all pain, all trouble, all sin, is a result of the Satanic hatred of the human race.

"In my name they shall cast out demons." They were to take Jesus' place. They were going out into the world and acting for Him.

I John 3:8, Jesus came to destroy the works of the devil. We are to act for Him today.

John 14:12, "Greater works than these shall ye do; because I go unto the Father. And whatsoever ye shall ask in my name, that will I do, that the Father may be glorified in the Son. If ye shall ask anything in my name, that will I do."

He is not talking about prayer. He is talking about casting out demons, about healing the sick, and miracles.

"Whatsoever ye shall demand in my name." That word "ask" means "demand." You are demanding as Peter did at the beautiful gate that morning when he said to the impotent man, " In the Name of Jesus Christ of Nazareth rise and walk."

The man was instantly healed. He was not a Christian. He had not accepted Christ. It is likely that the great multitudes who were healed, recorded in Acts 5, were made up of unsaved people.

The majority of the healings in the book of Acts were healings of sick people who had not yet become believers.

Read carefully Acts 5:12-16. Practically all these people were unsaved Jews.

In Acts 8:8-10 the power of God is again unveiled. All these miracles performed in Jesus' Name were upon the unsaved world.

The church has missed its greatest method of advertising. God's method of advertising was through miracles.

Divine healing has a large ministry with the unsaved today.

* * * * * * * * * * *

Christ was a miracle.

Christianity is Christ living in men today.

The Incarnation and the New Birth are both of God. Both are miracles.

Answered prayer is a miracle. When prayer does not produce miracles it is but empty words.

A miracle is God moving into the sense realm.

Don't condemn yourself for your doubts. Cure them by getting acquainted with your Father.

Confession always goes ahead of healing.

Don't watch symptoms – watch the Word, and be sure that your confession is bold and vigorous.

Don't listen to people. Act on the Word. Be a doer of the Word.

It is God speaking.

You are healed. The Word says you are.

Don't listen to the senses. Give the Word its place.

God cannot lie.

Chapter VII

GOD'S METHOD OF HEALING BABES IN CHRIST

S any among you sick?" There should be no sick among you because "By His stripes you are healed."

Because there has been no spiritual development or growth, and you are still babes in Christ, you are sick.

Healing for the Carnally Minded Man

Carnal means Sense-ruled.

The carnally minded man is a Christian who has not yet come to the place where the Word rules him and governs his thinking.

He is called "a babe in Christ," carnally minded, fleshly.

He is ruled by the flesh, by what he sees with his eyes, what he feels, hears, tastes, and smells.

He is a body-ruled, sense-governed child of God. He is a babe in Christ.

I Corinthians 3:1-3, "And, I, brethren, could not speak unto you as unto spiritual," that is, men whose spirits have gained the ascendancy over their thinking. Their spirit is recreated, but the unrenewed mind rules their spirit.

"I cannot speak unto you as men whose minds are subordinate to the Word of God." Their minds were not renewed. They were still babes.

Hebrews 5:11-14, "Of whom we have many things to say, and hard of interpretation, seeing ye are become dull of hearing."

How many believers fall under this admonition. They cannot understand the Word.

"For everyone that partaketh of milk is without experience of the Word of Righteousness, for he is a babe."

This "Word of Righteousness" is very little understood. They have never had an experience in living Righteousness.

What do we mean by that?

Righteousness means the ability to stand in the presence of the Father, or of demons, or of sickness and disease, without the sense of inferiority, condemnation, or of sin-consciousness.

Those who live Righteousness, or who know by the Word that they are the Righteousness of God in Christ, are absolute masters over circumstances, demons, and disease.

2 Corinthians 5:21, "Him who knew no sin, he made to be sin on our behalf; that we might become the righteousness of God in him."

You are having experience in the Word of Righteousness. You are finding that it is the Word that heals.

This ministry of the Word of God is the Word of Righteousness. It is the Word of Righteousness that sets men free, leads them out of Satan's dominion into the liberty and freedom of the sons of God.

How fearless they become. How mightily they speak.

14th verse, "But solid food is for fullgrown men, even those who by reason of use have their senses exercised to discern good and evil."

The believer described above has grown up into a spiritual life in Christ.

He has fed on the Word until the Word has transfigured him.

James 5:14-16 is God's method of healing the carnally minded, or the babes in Christ.

God, in great grace says, "Let him call for the elders of the church; and let them pray over him, anointing him with oil in the name of the Lord; and the prayer of faith shall save him that is sick, and the Lord shall raise him up and if he have committed sins, it shall be forgiven him. Confess therefore your sins one to another, and pray one for another, that ye may be healed. The supplication of a righteous man availeth much in its working."

Notice very carefully these facts. He cannot see that his disease was laid on Christ, but he can see the elders, hear their prayers, and feel the anointing oil upon his forehead. He can feel their hands upon his head.

He is living in the realm of the senses. Grace comes down and meets him in this realm.

If he had taken advantage of his privileges, he would have acted on I John 1:9, "If we confess our sins, he is faithful and righteous to forgive us our sins, and to cleanse us from all unrighteousness."

This scripture is to the Christian. Had that believer, that babe in Christ, taken advantage of his rights and privileges, he would have looked up and said, "Father, forgive me for the thing I have done which caused my sickness."

The Father would have forgiven him and healed him then.

But he has to see and feel before he can believe. He belongs to Thomas' class, "When I see, I will believe."

Practically all the faith that men had in Jesus before His death and Resurrection was Sense Knowledge faith.

They believed in things they saw and heard. They could not believe in a Resurrection. They had never seen a Resurrection.

They had seen Lazarus raised from the dead. He was simply raised, brought back to life again. He was not Resurrected; he died again.

Oh the grace of our Lord Jesus Christ that comes down to our level and meets us where we cannot apparently act on the Word because we are governed by the Senses.

Chapter VIII

HEALING IN REDEMPTION

W E have seen healing for the world in the Name of Jesus. We have seen healing for the carnally minded believer through the elders.

Now let us see healing for the man who enjoys the fulness, of his privileges in Christ.

Isaiah 53 is a preview of Jesus' public ministry and His Substitutionary Sacrifice.

It is a veiled prophecy, but it is revealed now through the Pauline Revelation as belonging to us.

Love's Good Pleasure

"He was despised, and rejected of men; a man of pains and acquainted with disease." He was a root out of dry ground. But He was precious to the Father, though condemned by the world.

"As one from whom men hide their face he was despised; and we esteemed him not. Surely he hath borne our sicknesses, and carried our diseases; yet we did esteem him stricken, smitten of God, and afflicted."

Isaiah 52:14, "Like as many were astonished at thee (his visage was so marred more than any man), and his form more than the sons of men."

The margin of the Cross-Reference Bible reads, "Men were dumbfounded at Him, for deformed was His appearance so as not to be a man, and his figure so as not to be human."

Or, "So shall many be amazed over Him. His visage was so marred, unlike to a man, and His form unlike the sons of men. His visage was so as not to be a man, and his figure no longer resembled a man."

He was made sin with our sin. He was under the dominion of Satan.

This is a description of Jesus' spirit, not His body.

He was made sick with our diseases and when those diseases came upon His precious spirit, He no longer resembled a man.

The heart cannot take it in. Reason stands dumb in the presence of statements like these.

"He was stricken, smitten of God, and afflicted."

It was God who laid our diseases upon Him. It was justice that demanded a recompense for our offenses.

"He was wounded for our transgressions, he was bruised for our iniquities; the chastisement of our peace was upon him; and with his stripes we are healed."

Sickness Is Spiritual

Now you can see this fact; that sickness was healed spiritually. God did not deal with sickness physically.

Disease today is spiritual. I have found that when I can prove, through the Word, that our diseases were laid on Jesus, and the sick man accepts that fact, he is instantly healed.

As long as we think that disease is purely physical, we will not get our deliverance.

But when we know it is spiritual, and it must be healed by the Word of God, for you remember He said, "He sent His Word and healed them," then healing becomes a reality.

"He was wounded for our transgressions." This was spiritual. "He was bruised for our iniquities." It was a spiritual bruising.

The wounds that the soldiers made did not take away sin, for if they had, sin would be a physical thing, a Sense Knowledge thing.

Human justice deals only with Sense evidences --- not what a man thinks, but what he says or does.

He endured sufferings that the Senses cannot understand.

They stand mute and helpless in the presence of this great spiritual tragedy that took place on Calvary.

"The chastisement of our peace was upon him; and with his stripes we are healed."

It was not the physical wounds made by the lictor. It was the stripes that justice laid upon His spirit.

"All we like sheep have gone astray; we have turned everyone to his own way; and Jehovah hath laid on him the iniquity of us all."

10th verse, "Yet it pleased Jehovah to bruise him; he hath made him sick." (Marginal rendering R. V.) Love could see humanity Redeemed. Faith could see a New Creation

He made Him sick with our sickness. We need not be sick. Only ignorance of our rights, or refusal to act upon the Word can keep us ill.

He made Him sin with our sin. We need not remain in sin. He became sin that we might become Righteous. He went to Hell that we might go to Heaven.

He was made weak that we might be made strong. He took our place, met every need, satisfied every claim of justice, and set us free.

If this be the case, sickness on the part of the believer is wrong, just as weakness and every other thing that Satan brought upon man is wrong, because He suffered to put it away.

Some Facts About the Supernatural Life

In the mind of the Father we are supermen. We are conquerors; we are overcomers.

1 John 5:4-5, "For whatsoever is begotten of God overcometh the world: and this is the victory that hath overcome the world, even our faith."

It was our faith that brought us into the family of conquerors.

"Who is he that overcometh the world, but he that believeth that Jesus is the Son of God?"

We believe that Jesus is the Son of God, that He died for our sins according to scripture and that He arose again for our justification.

We believe that the moment we take Him to be our Savior and confess Him as our Lord, God takes us to be His children and gives us Eternal Life.

This places us in the realm of conquerors. We are supermen and superwomen.

Believers Are Winners

Healing and victory are ours. They are ours without asking. All we need to do is to simply know it and praise Him for it.

Hebrews 4:14-16, "Having then a great high priest, who hath passed through the heavens, Jesus the Son of God, let us hold fast our confession."

Your old version reads, "profession."

We are to hold fast our confession. What is our confession? It is that we are New Creations, that sin has been put away, and that we are the Righteousness of God in Him.

We confess that "surely He has borne our sicknesses and carried our diseases."

Our confession is that He was stricken, smitten of God with our infirmities and weaknesses, and now by His stripes we are absolutely healed.

28

Sin and disease have been put away, and in the Name of Jesus we have dominion over Satan and the work of his hands.

In His Name we cast out demons. In His Name we lay hands on the sick and they do recover.

If we can cast out demons, we can also command the demon Disease to leave our bodies, for disease was brought there by a demon and is being developed by a demon.

We say, "In Jesus' Name, Demon, leave this body." That demon is under obligation to the Name of Jesus to obey.

When Jesus arose from the dead, He arose because we with Him, had conquered Satan.

Colossians 2:15, "Having despoiled the principalities and the powers, he made a show of them openly, triumphing over them in it."

Jesus' triumph is our triumph. Jesus' victory is our victory. He did nothing for Himself. It was all for us. Today we are more than conquerors through Him who loved us.

We should never talk about our diseases. When we tell our troubles to people it is always to get their sympathy.

That trouble came from the adversary. When we tell our troubles, we are giving our testimony of Satan's ability to get us into difficulty.

When we talk about our diseases, we are glorifying the adversary who had the ability to put that disease upon us.

When we confess our lack of strength or ability, we confess that Satan has so blinded us that we cannot enjoy our rights and privileges.

Psalm 27:1, "Jehovah is my light and my salvation; Whom shall I fear? Jehovah is the strength of my life: Of whom shall I be afraid?"

God has made Him to be wisdom unto us. He has made Him to be Redemption unto us.

If this be true, then Satan has no right to reign over us with sickness, disease, weakness, or failure.

Every time we talk of our troubles, we glorify the being who put the troubles upon us.

Our confession should be that God is today our strength, our wisdom, our complete and perfect Redemption, our Sanctification, and our Righteousness.

We are the Righteousness of God in Him. We can do all things in Him who strengthens us.

Today the Name of Jesus in our lips can conquer disease and sickness. That Name can bring courage and victory to the defeated and whipped.

* * * * * * * * * * *

The prayer of unbelief never gives faith.

When you pray for faith, you confess your unbelief.

This increases your doubts, for the prayer is never heard.

The doubter often prays for things already his own.

God has blessed him with every spiritual blessing that governs every spiritual need.

Redemption has never been seen as a reality. It is a theory, a creed, a doctrine.

Few expect experimental evidence of it.

Satan has taken advantage of our ignorance of Redemption and put disease upon us, holding us in bondage.

The defeated one holds his master in bondage.

The believer is Satan's master.

Chapter IX

METHODS OF HEALING

HERE are five ways by which healings are obtained through the Word. It will be interesting to notice them.

In a previous chapter I have called your attention to the fact that the early church used healing as a means of advertising the Gospel as well as blessing the people.

John 14:13-14 can be used in this connection. "And whatsoever ye shall ask (or demand), in my name, that will I do, that the Father may be glorified in the Son. If ye shall ask anything in my name, that will I do."

If a pain comes you say, "In the Name of Jesus Christ, leave my body." The pain must go. You are the master of your own body. You rule it.

You have a right to freedom from pain or sickness. In that Name you command it to leave. You are not demanding it of the Father, because the Father has given you authority over these demoniacal forces.

You can use the Name to break the power of the adversary over the unsaved and make it easy for them to accept Christ. In that name, "They that believe shall lay hands on the sick and they shall recover."

Every believer should understand this clearly, that he has a right to perfect deliverance from the hand of his enemy in that Name.

Second Method

A second method is found in Mark 16:18. "In my name ... they shall lay hands on the sick, and they shall recover."

The believer has the nature of God in him. He has the life of God in him. The Spirit dwells in him.

It is that power within him that goes out through his hands in the Name of Jesus and heals the sick.

Sometimes it is accompanied by manifestations. The person feels the life of God go pouring through his body.

Other times there is no manifestation.

It makes no difference whether or not there is any Sense witness. "They that believe shall lay hands on the sick and they shall recover."

The same power that is in him can be exercised in the Name of

Jesus for a sick one in a distant place. The moment he prays in that Name, God's healing power reaches out to that one and he is healed.

Third Method

A third method is for the carnal believer, that is, the believer who is governed by the senses and not by the Word.

1 Corinthians 3:1-3 calls him a babe in Christ. James says (5:14), "Is any among you sick? Let him call for the elders of the church; and let them pray over him, anointing him with oil in the name of the Lord: and the prayer of faith shall save him that is sick, and the Lord shall raise him up; and if he have committed sins, it shall be forgiven him."

This scripture is not for full-grown believers, but for those who have never developed their spiritual life so as to take their places in Christ. It is for those who must depend on others to pray for them.

Fourth Method

A fourth method of healing is found in John 16:23-24. "And in that day ye shall ask me nothing. Verily, verily, I say unto you, If ye shall ask anything of the Father, he will give it you in my name. Hitherto have ye asked nothing in my name; ask, and ye shall receive, that your joy may be made full."

Every believer has a right to ask the Father for healing or any other blessing and if he asks in the Name of Jesus, he has the absolute guarantee that the Father will hear and answer his petition.

Fifth Method

A fifth method of healing is found in Matthew 18:18-20.

"If two of you shall agree on earth as touching anything that they shall ask, it shall be done for them of my Father who is in heaven. For where two or three are gathered together in my name, there am I in the midst of them."

Where two are united, and are demanding in Jesus' Name the healing of loved ones, prayer is bound to be answered. God watches over His Word to make it good.

Healing in Redemption

There is another method of healing which I believe to be the best.

Isaiah 53:3-5, "Surely he hath borne our sicknesses, and carried our diseases; yet, we did esteem him stricken, smitten of God, and afflicted." He was smitten with our diseases.

"He was wounded for our transgressions, he was bruised for our iniquities; the chastisement of our peace was upon him; and with his stripes we are healed."

Here is the absolute statement of fact that by His stripes we are healed.

1 Pet. 2:24, "Who his own self bare our sins in his body upon the tree, that we, having died unto sins, might live unto righteousness; by whose stripes ye were healed."

Matthew 8:16-17, "That it might be fulfilled which was spoken through Isaiah the prophet, saying, Himself took our infirmities, and bare our diseases."

These scriptures prove that healing is ours. We simply know that by His stripes we are healed. We thank the Father for our perfect deliverance. It is not necessary that we pray, or ask the Father to heal us.

We know that He said, "By His stripes ye were healed." The afflictions in our bodies were laid upon Jesus. He bore them. We do not need to bear them.

All we need to do is to recognize and accept that fact. We refuse to allow disease in our bodies. We are healed.

Every believer should thoroughly understand that his healing was consummated in Christ.

It would mean the end of chronic troubles in the body of the believer.

Chapter X

JESUS, THE HEALER

F it were not for this thing you call sin-consciousness, I would have faith. If I had faith, I would have my healing. "But the Word does not seem real to me. I read it, and I say, 'By His stripes I am healed' and yet in my mind I hear another voice saying, 'But the pain is still there.'

"I find that I am giving two testimonies continually, one with my lips and another with my intellect."

We should fully understand this: no matter what one's standing is in heaven, if he has no faith in it, it does him no good.

No matter what a man's privileges are, if the hand of faith is paralyzed he cannot take hold of them.

As long as he is ruled by sin-consciousness, he has no sense of Redemption. He is under condemnation. Satan rules him.

As long as Satan rules, faith will be shriveled and undeveloped.

All through the Pauline Revelation, from Romans through Hebrews, a complete Redemption is taught.

There is a perfect Redemption. Satan is conquered.

Hebrews 2:14, "Since then the children are sharers in flesh and blood, he also himself in like manner partook of the same; that through death he might bring to nought him that had the authority of death, that is, the devil."

He is stripped of his authority.

Revelation 1:18, Jesus triumphantly says, "I am He that was dead, and behold I am alive forevermore; and I have the keys of death and hades."

Satan was put to nought; his ability was paralyzed.

Colossians 2:15, "He put off from himself the principalities and powers, and made a show of them, openly triumphing over them in it." (Marginal rendering R. V.)

Satan, then, has no dominion over us.

Romans, 6:14, "Sin shall not have dominion over you."

If Redemption does not deliver us from sin-consciousness, it is no better than Judaism. If it cannot free us now from condemnation, God and Christ have failed; Satan has become the master.

If sin-consciousness rules, acting on the Word is impossible. Faith is a withered flower where sin-consciousness rules.

The problem of faith, then, is to get rid of sin-consciousness. The Word is the only cure. It declares that we are Redeemed.

Ephesians 1:7, "In whom we have our redemption through his blood, the remission of our sins."

If we have been Redeemed, Satan's dominion is broken, and we are free.

Not only has a perfect Redemption been accomplished, but provision for a perfect recreation has been made.

2 Corinthians 5:17, "Wherefore if any man is in Christ, he is a new creation: the old things are passed away; behold, they are become new. But all things are of God, who reconciled us to himself through Christ, and gave unto us the ministry of reconciliation."

There is a complete recreation and a complete reconciliation.

If God has recreated us, we are not under bondage to the things of the old creation.

If a man has been recreated, it is God's own work. He did it through the Holy Spirit and His own Word.

That New Creation is effected by the impartation of God's own nature.

2 Peter 1:4, we become partakers of the divine nature. We are actually born from above. The old sin nature has gone, and a new nature, which is free from condemnation, has taken its place.

Romans 8:1, 33, "There is therefore now no condemnation to them that are in Christ Jesus."

We have been made free from the law of sin and of death. "Who shall lay anything to the charge of God's elect? Who is he that condemneth?" God has justified, or declared us Righteous.

The word "Justify" means "to make Righteous." Righteousness is the ability to stand in the Father's presence without the sense of guilt, sin, or inferiority.

We stand there as though sin had never been.

If Redemption does not mean that, if the New Creation does not give that, God has failed.

The New Creation must be as free from sin as Adam was before he committed sin, or God has failed in His Redemptive work.

Someone says, "What about 1 John 1:6?"

"If we say we have no sin, we deceive ourselves, and the truth is not in us."

He is speaking of broken fellowship. If a man says he has fellowship with the Father when he is living under condemnation, he is telling a lie.

"If we say we have fellowship with Him and walk in the darkness, we lie, and do not the truth."

Every man who is living in broken fellowship is walking in darkness.

1 John 1:9, "If we confess our sins, He is faithful and Righteous to

forgive us our sins, and to cleanse us from all unrighteousness."

If we say that we have not sinned when we are living out of fellowship, we are telling an untruth.

"But if we do sin, we have an Advocate with the Father, Jesus Christ the Righteous."

Ephesians 2:10, "We are His workmanship."

He not only made us New Creations, but He made us Righteous.

Romans 3:26, "That He might Himself be Righteous and the Righteousness of him that hath faith in Jesus." (R. V. margin.)

This declares that He has become the Righteousness of the man who has faith in Jesus as Savior.

If God has become our Righteousness, we have a legal standing in His presence.

1 Corinthians 1:30 tells us that He was made unto us Righteousness. "But of Him are ye in Christ Jesus, who was made unto us wisdom from God, and righteousness and sanctification, and redemption."

Then we have God as our Righteousness and Jesus as our Righteousness.

Romans 4:25 (literal translation), "He was delivered up on the account of our trespasses and was raised, because we stood Righteous before Him."

Roman 5:1, "being therefore declared Righteous by faith we have peace with God through our Lord Jesus Christ."

2 Corinthians 5:21, "Him who knew no sin, God made to be sin on our behalf; that we might become the Righteousness of God in Him."

He not only becomes our Righteousness, but now He also makes us His Righteousness by a New Birth, a recreation.

We stand before Him reconciled, without condemnation in fellowship with Him.

If the scripture means anything, it means exactly what it says.

The Believer has a legal right to stand in the Father's presence without condemnation. If He can do that, then acting on the Word is possible.

If acting on the Word is possible, everything that belongs to us in Christ becomes available at once.

* * * * * * * * * * *

When Jesus arose from the dead, He left an eternally defeated Satan behind Him.

Always think of Satan as the eternally defeated one.

Chapter X1

THE DISEASE PROBLEM

THIS is Jesus' spiritual ministry. It began on the cross. Isaiah 53:3-5.

"He was despised, and rejected of men; a man of pains and acquainted with disease: and as one from whom men hide their face He was despised; and we esteemed Him not. Surely He hath borne our sicknesses and carried our diseases; yet we did esteem Him stricken, smitten of God, and afflicted. But He was wounded for our transgressions, He was bruised for our iniquities; the chastisement of our peace was upon Him; and with His stripes we are healed.'"

The disciples could not see it when they looked upon the thorn-crowned Man of Galilee.

He was then bearing our sicknesses and diseases.

10th verse, "Yet it pleased Jehovah to bruise Him. He hath made Him sick."

He made Him sin with our sins, sick with our sicknesses.

Isaiah 52:14, "His visage was marred more than any man." It was so marred that He no longer looked like a man.

That was not His physical body.

God could not look on His soul. "When God made His soul an offering for sin." He was stricken, smitten of God and afflicted.

It was God who laid our diseases on Him. He was smitten by Justice, because He was our Substitute.

He was bruised for our iniquities. The chastisement of our peace was upon Him, and "with His stripes we are healed."

It was not the physical stripes upon His back made by the Roman lictor, but the stripes that God put upon Him with our diseases when He was judged and cast out in our stead.

Matthew 8:17, "That it might be fulfilled which was spoken through Isaiah the prophet, saying, Himself took our infirmities, and bare our diseases."

Our infirmities are our little mental quirks, the things that make us disagreeable and unpleasant to people. These are largely infirmities of the mind.

He bore them all. What He bore, we do not need to bear. What He took upon Himself, we need not suffer.

We have come to believe that it is just as wrong for a believer to bear his sickness when Jesus bore it, as it is for him to bear his sins when Christ bore them.

We have no right to live in sin and to bear those hateful habits that make life a curse, because Christ bore them.

It was wrong for Him to bear them if we are going to bear them too.

It is wrong for us to have sickness and disease in our bodies when God laid those diseases on Jesus.

He became sick with our diseases, that we might be healed.

He knew no sickness until He was made sick with our diseases.

The object of His sin-bearing was to make Righteous the ones who believe on Him.

The object of disease-bearing was to make well the ones who believe in Him as the disease-bearer.

His sin-bearing made Righteousness sure to the New Creation. His disease-bearing makes healing sure to the New Creation.

He took our sins and made us Righteous. He took our diseases, and made us well. He took our infirmities and gave us His strength. He exchanged His strength for our weakness, His success for our failings.

Disease Is Not the Will of the Father

We understand that disease is broken ease, broken fellowship with heaven. Disease is pain, weakness, loss of ability to bless and help.

It makes slaves of the people who care for the sick. The loved ones who are up night and day working over the sick ones are robbed of joy and rest.

Sickness is not of love, and God is love. Disease is a robber. It steals health; it steals happiness. It steals money we need for other things. Disease is an enemy.

Look at what it has stolen from that Tuberculosis patient. It came upon him in the midst of young manhood, and has made him a burden to his family, filled him with anxiety and doubt, fear and pain. It has robbed him of his faith.

See what disease has done to that woman; it has robbed her of her beauty and her joy and love. She is no longer able to fill the place of a mother or wife. All this is of the devil.

Jesus said (Luke 13:1-17) that disease was of Satan.

"And behold, a woman that had a spirit of infirmity eighteen years; and she was bowed together, and could in no wise lift herself up ...

38

And ought not this woman, being a daughter of Abraham, whom Satan had bound, lo, these eighteen years, to have been loosed from this bond?"

She was Satan-bound.

Acts 10:38 tells us that Jesus went about doing good, and healing all that were oppressed of the devil.

From the beginning to the end of Jesus' public ministry He was combating Satan.

His battle was not with men, but entirely with demons who indwelt men.

It was the devil who used the High priesthood to stir up the strife which finally nailed Jesus to the cross.

Don't tell anyone that disease is the will of love. It is the will of hate; it is the will of Satan.

If disease becomes the will of love, love has turned to hatred.

If disease is the will of God, heaven will be filled with disease and sickness.

Jesus was the express will of the Father; He went about healing the sick.

Disease and sickness are never the will of the Father. To believe that they are, is to be disillusioned by the adversary.

If healing had not been in the plan of Redemption, it would not have been in the substitutionary chapter of Isaiah 53.

If healing had not been in Redemption, the Father would not have taught it in His Word.

Jesus healed all who came to Him, Jews and Gentiles alike. He was carrying out the will of the Father. He was the will of the Father.

Chapter XII

MADE WELL IN CHRIST

O matter from what angle you look at Christianity, it is a miracle. The most amazing miracle is the New Creation. We have never been able to get at the heart of it. We have stood outside as spectators and looked at it from its various angles.

A man becomes a New Creation by receiving the very Life and Nature of God.

Take these scriptures as illustrations.

Colossians 2:13, "And you, being dead through your trespasses and the uncircumcision of the flesh, you, I say, did He make alive together with Him, having been gracious to us in all our trespasses."

We have been made alive together with Him.

12th verse, "Wherein ye were also raised with Him through faith in the working of God, who raised Him from the dead."

This is the legal aspect of the New Creation and everything that is legally ours can become a vital reality.

In the mind of the Father, we were made alive with Christ.

When He was made alive in spirit, we were made alive in spirit.

This becomes a reality to us when we personally accept Christ as Savior and confess Him as Lord. The life of God comes into our spirits and recreates us.

Ephesians 2:1-2, "And you did He make alive, when ye were dead through your trespasses and sins."

This can be called the miracle of Christianity, an actual New Creation.

There would be more pleasure in old age than in youth if we did not fear it.

We dread it because of the haunting fear of pain and disease and the struggle with death.

Life and Death

A few facts about life and death may be helpful to us.

Spiritual Death is the parent of physical death. There was no physical death until Adam died spiritually.

There was no death in the original blueprints of Creation. We know that at the end of this age, death will be swallowed up of Immortality.

1 Corinthians 15:26, "The last enemy that shall be abolished is death."

There is going to be a deathless eternity. Why can't there be a sickless present? I believe it is the will of the Father that the church be as free from sickness as it is from sin.

Death is an enemy. Weakness and disease are enemies. Death is not only the enemy of man, but it is also the enemy of God.

2 Timothy 1:10 tells us that in the Resurrection of the Lord Jesus, death lost its dominion.

"But hath now been manifested by the appearing of our Savior Christ Jesus, who abolished death, and brought life and immortality to light through the gospel."

He did two things: He brought Life and Immortality to us, and He abolished the dominion of death.

When He arose from the dead, He had conquered death personally.

He conquered death in Lazarus. He conquered death in the widow's son. He was the Lord of life.

Revelation 20:14 , "And death and Hades were cast into the lake of fire."

Revelation 21:4, "And He shall wipe away every tear from their eyes; and death shall be no more; neither shall there be mourning, nor crying, nor pain, anymore."

It will be the end of death. This promise of the final destruction of death has in it a suggestion that there is in the plan of Redemption, something to give us assurance of a sickless life, until our bodies wear out and mortality wins without a struggle.

"He was despised, and rejected of men; a man of pains, and acquainted with sickness: and as one from whom men hide their face He was despised; and we esteemed Him not.

"Surely He hath borne our diseases, and carried our sicknesses; yet we did esteem Him stricken, smitten of God, and afflicted. But He was wounded for our transgressions, He was bruised for our iniquities; the chastisement of our peace was upon Him; and with His stripes we are healed."

10th verse, "Yet it pleased Jehovah to bruise Him; He hath put Him to grief," or "made Him sick."

12th verse, "Because He poured out His soul unto death, and was numbered with the transgressors: Yet He bare the sin of many, and made intercession for the transgressors."

That is His High Priestly ministry now at the right hand of the Father.

We can see in this whole program that heads up in these words: "With His stripes we are healed," that the sin and disease problems have been settled.

As surely as Jesus was our sin substitute as described in 2 Corinthians 5:21, so surely have we become the Righteousness of God in Him.

The object of His being made sick with our diseases was that we might be perfectly healed with His Life.

There is no escaping the fact that as surely as He dealt with the sin problem, He dealt with the disease problem.

Hebrews 9:26, "But now once at the end of the ages hath He been manifested to put away sin by the sacrifice of Himself."

Hebrews 10:12, "But He, when He had offered one sacrifice for sins forever, sat down on the right hand of God."

He put sin away that we might be Born Again, become New Creations, that the sin nature which had held us in bondage to the adversary should be eradicated and that the nature of God should take its place.

It is the New Nature that settles the sin problem for us individually.

The problem of sins is settled. The things we did before we accepted Christ are wiped out as though they had never been.

Now we are in the Family. We are the Righteousness of God in Him.

Hebrews 10:38, "But my righteous one shall live by faith: And if he shrink back, my soul hath no pleasure in him."

The New Creation is called the Righteousness of God. He is the Righteousness of God.

His standing with the Father is just like Jesus' standing. But if he sins, he has an Advocate with the Father, Jesus Christ the Righteous.

He loses the sense of Righteousness when he sins, but Jesus, the Righteous One, intercedes for him and restores his lost fellowship and sense of Righteousness.

Fellowship and Healing

1 John 1:9, "If we confess our sins, He is faithful and Righteous to forgive us our sins, and to cleanse us from all unrighteousness."

This restores his fellowship, brings him back into full communion with the Father.

Now by the same token, after one has been healed, (because "By His stripes we are healed") in the mind of God he is just as much healed of disease as he is healed of sin.

If, after he has been healed of disease, the adversary puts upon him some other disease or infirmity, all he needs to do is to follow the procedure that he followed when he broke fellowship with the Father spiritually.

Sickness is breaking fellowship with the Father physically. As he can get restoration of fellowship and a restoration of his sense of Righteousness by confessing his sins and by the advocacy of Jesus Christ, he can get his physical healing.

Disease of the spirit is the thing that keeps one from his healing.

Diseases of the spirit are doubts, fears, sin-consciousness, a sense of inferiority, fear of unworthiness, and a sense of unfitness to stand in God's presence.

The blood of Jesus Christ, God's Son, cleanses from all this, the moment he acknowledges his sin.

Forgiveness means the absolute wiping out of everything he has confessed, as though he had never committed the act.

2 Corinthians 5:4-5, "For indeed we that are in this tabernacle do groan, being burdened; not for that we would be unclothed, but that we would be clothed upon, that what is mortal may be swallowed up of life. Now He that wrought us for this very thing is God, who gave unto us the earnest of the Spirit."

The Greek word here for life is "Zoe." It means Eternal Life, Resurrection Life.

In other words, it means that the life of the Son of God, Eternal Life, can absolutely dominate, rule, swallow up, and control our physical lives.

If this be true, then sickness is absolutely defeated, physical weakness is eliminated, and Psalm 27:1 is a reality.

"Jehovah is my light and my salvation; whom, shall I fear? Jehovah is the strength of my life; Of whom shall I be afraid?"

Light is knowledge. Jesus is the light of the world. He who walks in that light will not stumble as one who walks in darkness, because he will have the Light of Life.

John 8:12, "I am the light of the world: he that followeth me shall not walk in the darkness, but shall have the light of life."

The Word will be his lamp, his light, his salvation. That is true deliverance; that is Redemption.

Psalm 119:105, "Thy Word is a lamp unto my feet, and a light unto my path." It is deliverance from the things that are not in the Father's will.

You cannot for a moment believe that mortality is in the Will of

43

the Father.

Mortality means weakness, sickness, death. You cannot conceive of disease and sickness being the will of the Father.

"Jehovah is my light and my salvation." This means salvation from sickness, disease, and weakness of the physical body.

Fear will no longer dominate your life.

If a man could be delivered from fear of weakness, death, or pain, he would be a conqueror.

Redemption planned that very thing, that these bodies of ours should never be subject to disease after we are Born Again.

Someone says, "What about Paul's thorn in the flesh?"

That was not sickness. It was a demon interfering with his public ministry in his speech, making him stammer. It had nothing to do with disease.

All that foolish talk about Luke being Paul's physician is not true. Physicians were sorcerers. They belonged to the spiritualistic group.

The Greek word "Pharmacia" from which we get "pharmacist" is the word for sorcerer.

In 2 Corinthians 4:10 Paul says, "Always bearing about in the body the dying of Jesus, that the life also of Jesus may be manifested in our body. For we who live are always delivered unto death for Jesus' sake."

Why? They lived in the constant fear of stoning, of being thrown to the lions, or being burned at the stake.

"That the life of Jesus may be manifested in our mortal flesh," is a startling statement; God's life reigning in our physical bodies.

Psalm 27:1, "Jehovah is the strength of my life; Of whom shall I be afraid?"

These mortal bodies, these death-doomed bodies of ours, now have the strength of God, the life of God.

Jesus' Life is imparted to our physical bodies. That is not healing. That is preservation from sickness. That is protection. That is the strength, and power, and ability of God in our physical bodies.

* * * * * * * * * * *

Don't try to get your healing.

God has given it to you.

Don't try to believe. You are a believer and all things are yours.

Don't talk doubt. It breeds more doubt.

44

Chapter XIII

DESTROYING THE WORKS
OF THE DEVIL

NE of the strongest scriptures in connection with healing is Romans 8:11: "But if the Spirit of Him that raised up Jesus from the dead dwelleth in you, He that raised up Christ Jesus from the dead shall give life also to your mortal bodies through His Spirit that dwelleth in you."

This is physical healing. This is the Holy Spirit, taking the life of God and making it efficacious in our physical bodies, making it health, and strength, and life to us.

This same Holy Spirit who raised the dead body of Jesus is now working in our death-doomed bodies, making them perfect – sickless and sinless.

1 John 3:8, "He that doeth sin is of the devil; for the devil sinneth from the beginning. To this end was the Son of God manifested, that He might destroy the works of the devil."

Jesus did His part of destroying the works of the devil. After He left the earth, He sent the Holy Spirit, and gave us the use of His own Name and this wonderful Revelation, the New Testament, that we, His representatives here on the earth, might go on destroying the works of the devil.

The sin, the sickness, and the diseases that are in the church today are there because of our not taking our places in Christ.

They are prevalent in the church today because we have never been exercised to do the work that Jesus said we were to do.

Do you think He would have given us John 14:12-14 if we were not to use it?

"Verily, verily, I say unto you, He that believeth on me, the works that I do shall he do also; and greater works than these shall he do; because I go unto the Father."

He meant that we should do greater works than He did, because there are a greater number of us.

Our work is that of destroying the works of the adversary. The weapon we are to use is found in the thirteenth and fourteenth verses.

"And whatsoever ye shall ask in my name, that will I do, that the Father may be glorified in the Son. If ye shall ask anything in my name, that will I do."

That word "Ask" means "Demand."

His Name is to be used in the sense that we see it used in Acts 3 by Peter who spoke to the impotent man at the gate of the temple saying, "In the name of Jesus Christ of Nazareth, walk."

This is not prayer. This is casting out demons in that Name. There is healing for the sick in that Name.

There is power to break disease and sickness in the hearts and lives of men in that Name.

Can that Name of Jesus keep us from sickness? Can it keep us from want? Can it keep us from poverty, fear, and the dread of hunger and cold?

Can that Name be used just as Jesus suggested in Mark 16:18?

"And these signs shall accompany them that believe: in my name shall they cast out demons; they shall speak with new tongues; they shall take up serpents, and if they drink any deadly thing, it shall in no wise hurt them; they shall lay hands on the sick, and they shall recover."

The early church was utterly independent of circumstances. I don't mean the whole church. I mean the apostles who understood fully the use of the Name of Jesus.

Men could be sick then by breaking fellowship and because of lack of knowledge, just as they can be today.

The early church, that is the Gentile portion of it, had never had any Revelation from God.

It was utterly raw material.

The Jews were in worse condition. They were Covenant breakers, as the modern church is.

The most difficult to deal with today are the most religious. If there was sickness in the early church, it was to be expected, because they bad no precedent, no examples ahead of them.

Jesus came to destroy the works of the devil. We are His instruments to do His work.

We are to destroy sickness in the church. Our new slogan is: "No more sickness in the body of Christ."

His Word is to become a reality in the lives of men.

The fact that He bore our sins and put sin away by the sacrifice of Himself, and that He made provision for the remission of all we have ever done or said, proves that we should not be sick or in bondage to sin.

He made the sacrifice for sins, the things we had done as a result of the sin nature.

The New Birth wipes out everything we have ever done.

2 Corinthians 5:17, "Wherefore if any man is in Christ, he is a new creature: the old things are passed away; behold, they are become new."

Romans 8:1 becomes a reality. "There is therefore now no condemnation to them that are in Christ Jesus."

The people who are in Christ Jesus are sin free, disease free, condemnation free.

Let us then, arise, take our place, and go out and carry this message of deliverance and victory to others.

It is very important that we grasp clearly 1 John 5:13. "These things have I written unto you, that ye may know that ye have eternal life, even unto you that believe on the name of the Son of God."

We have God's nature which gives us a perfect fellowship with the Father, a perfect right to use His Name, a perfect deliverance and freedom from Satan's dominion.

2 Peter 1:4, "Whereby He hath granted unto us His precious and exceeding great promises; that through these ye may become partakers of the divine nature."

John 14:13-14, "If ye shall ask anything in my name, that will I do."

Romans 6:14, "For sin shall not have dominion over you."

If sin cannot lord it over you, disease cannot lord it over you, because they come from the same source.

The nature and life of God that has come into you will give you life and health.

Psalm 91:16, "With long life will I satisfy him, And show him my salvation."

We all admit that the ninety-first Psalm belongs to the church. It could not apply to the Jew, but it does apply to us.

"He will cover thee with His pinions, And under His wings shalt thou take refuge: His truth (or Word) is a shield and a buckler. Thou shalt not be afraid for the terror by night, Nor for the arrow that flieth by day; For the pestilence that walketh in darkness, Nor for the destruction that wasteth at noonday. A thousand shall fall at thy side, And ten thousand at thy right hand; But it shall not come nigh thee."

There is protection from earthquakes, from cyclones, pestilence, from sickness, from war.

This thing puts us into the realm of the supernatural. We are linked up with Christ so that He said, "I am the vine, and ye are

47

the branches." John 15:5.

The life in the vine is in the branch. As soon as the branch is wounded, the vine pours life into the wounded branch so it can go on bearing fruit.

So the life of God pours into the body of Christ and heals the members of sickness, disease, and want, so they can go on bearing fruit to the glory of God.

Worry and fear poison the blood stream. Faith in the Lord Jesus purifies it.

* * * * * * * * * * *

Disease is defeated by your confession of the Word.

Disease gains the ascendency when you confess the testimony of your senses.

Satan is whipped with words.

You are healed with words.

Make your lips do their duty. Fill them with His Word.

Chapter XIV

THE ABUNDANT LIFE

HRISTIANITY is a living reality. John 10:10, "I came that they may have life, and may have it abundantly." It is the abundance of life that gives healing, strength, and energy. 1 Peter 5:7, "Casting all your anxiety upon Him, for He careth for you."

This means that in the mind of the Father there has come an end to worry, fear, and doubt.

The work of the adversary has been destroyed.

Exodus 23:25-26 was given to the Jews under the First Covenant, but it may become a living, sweet reality to us: "And ye shall serve Jehovah your God, and He will bless thy bread, and thy water; and I will take sickness away from the midst of thee. There shall none cast her young, nor be barren, in thy land; the number of thy days I will fulfill."

Is our Covenant as good as that?

Philippians 4:19, "And my God shall supply every need of yours according to His riches unveiled in Christ Jesus." (Lit. trans.)

Philippians 4:13, "I can do all things in Him that strengtheneth me."

Philippians 4:11, "Not that I speak in respect of want: for I have learned, in whatsoever state I am, therein to be independent of circumstances." (20th Century trans.)

We rise into the realm of the supernatural, absolute overcomers, perfect victors in Christ.

Is it any wonder that Paul, at the close of the eighth chapter of Romans declares, "Nay in all these things we are more than conquerors?" (37th verse.)

There is nothing that can separate us from the love of God as unveiled in Christ Jesus, our Lord.

Romans 8:32, "He that spared not His own Son, but delivered Him up for us all, how shall He not also with Him freely give us all things?"

We stand upon the mount of victory. Now we can say, "There is no more sickness in the body of Christ."

His Word is a reality in the lives of the sons of God. We are going out today to destroy the works of the enemy in the bodies, minds, and spirits of men.

There are several methods of healing, but the one that stands first in the mind of the Spirit is found in Isaiah 53:4-6: "Surely He hath borne our sicknesses, and carried our diseases, yet we did esteem Him stricken, smitten of God, and afflicted."

He was stricken and smitten with our diseases.

"But He was wounded for our transgressions, He was bruised for our iniquities; the chastisement of our peace was upon Him; and with His stripes we are healed."

Sin and sickness are one in the mind of the Father. Anything that touches the man and injures the man, God is against. Disease touches the man, and God laid it upon Jesus. Sin touches the man, and God laid it upon Jesus.

"All we like sheep have gone astray; we have turned everyone to his own way; and Jehovah hath laid on Him the iniquity of us all."

10th. verse, "He hath made Him sick."

When He declares that by His stripes we are healed, that means our freedom from sickness.

That is our receipt in full for a sickless and sinless life, for sin and disease shall not have dominion over us.

We take what belongs to us as sons and daughters of God.

We know that sin shall not have dominion over us. Romans 6:14.

1 John 1:7: We know that the blood of Jesus Christ cleanses from sin. "But if we walk in the light, as He is in the light, we have fellowship one with another, and the blood of Jesus His Son cleanseth us from all sin."

If we have committed sin, we have an Advocate with the Father.

1 John 2:1, "My little children, these things write I unto you that ye may not sin. And if any man sin, we have an Advocate with the Father, Jesus Christ the righteous."

We know that if we confess our sins, He will forgive us and cleanse us.

1 John 1:9, "If we confess our sins, He is faithful and righteous to forgive us our sins, and to cleanse us from all unriohteousness."

We come to Him with all our diseases knowing that all those diseases were laid on Jesus.

Then it is not right that we should bear them. The adversary has no right to put diseases on us, because they were laid on Christ.

I can say to the Father, "Do you see what the adversary has done in my body? In the Name of Jesus I take deliverance from this thing with which Satan has afflicted me."

I whisper to my heart, "By His stripes I am healed." The pain must go.

Multitudes are being healed like that today through our ministry.

We can be just as free from diseases as we are free from bad habits, and after all, the habit of sickness is like any other unclean habit.

There is provision made for a perfect healing. None of us need suffer from the hand of the enemy. Your deliverance is in the Redemptive work of Christ.

Chapter XV

THE ORIGIN OF SICKNESS

The Cruelty of Nature

T is hard for us to understand that the laws that are governing the earth very largely came into being with the Fall of man, and with the curse upon the earth.

It is because of this, that many accuse God of the accidents that take place, of the sickness and death of loved ones, of storms and catastrophes, of earthquakes and floods that continually occur.

All these natural laws, as we understand them, were set aside by Jesus whenever it was necessary to bless humanity.

They came with the Fall. Their author is Satan, and when Satan is finally eliminated from human contact, or rather, from the earth, these laws will stop functioning.

The Origin of Sickness

Jesus' description of the Father and His declaration that "He that hath seen me hath seen the Father," makes it impossible for us for a moment to accept the teaching that disease and sickness are of God.

The Father's very nature refutes the argument that He would use sickness to discipline us or to deepen our piety.

Jesus plainly taught us in Luke 13 in speaking of the woman with the infirmity, that disease is of the adversary.

"And ought not this woman, being a daughter of Abraham, whom Satan had bound, lo, these eighteen years, to have been loosed from this bond on the day of the sabbath?"

If you will read carefully the Four Gospels, you will notice that Jesus was continually casting demons out of sick people, breaking Satan's dominion over the lives of men and women.

In Acts 10:38 Peter tells us, "Jesus of Nazareth, how God anointed him with the Holy Spirit and with power: who went about doing good, and healing all that were oppressed of the devil; for God was with him."

In the great commission Jesus said, "These signs shall accompany them that believe: in my name shall they cast out demons; they shall speak with new tongues; they shall take up serpents, and if they drink any deadly thing, it shall in no wise hurt them; they shall lay hands on the sick, and they shall recover."

There is no such thing as the separation of disease and sickness from Satan. Disease came with the Fall of man.

You cannot conceive of sickness in the Garden of Eden before Adam sinned. The Fall was of the adversary. Sickness and sin have the same origin.

Jesus' attitude toward sickness was an uncompromising warfare with Satan. He healed all who were sick. No one ever came to Him who did not receive immediate deliverance.

Jesus' attitude toward sin and His attitude toward sickness were identical. He dealt with sickness as He dealt with demons.

We have been driven to the conclusion that if disease and sickness are of the devil, and we have found that they are, then there is only one attitude that the believer can take in regard to them: we must follow in Jesus' footsteps and deal with disease as Jesus dealt with it.

How God Dealt With Disease Under the First Covenant

When Israel came out of Egypt, she was God's own Covenant people. As soon as that nation had crossed the Red Sea and started toward its homeland, the angel of the Covenant said to Moses (Exodus 15:26):

"If thou wilt diligently hearken to the voice of Jehovah thy God, and wilt do that which is right in his eyes, and wilt give ear to his commandments, and keep all his statutes, I will permit none of the diseases upon thee, which I have permitted upon the Egyptians: for I am Jehovah that healeth thee."

The student of Hebrew will recognize that I have taken liberty to translate literally that expression "I will put none of these diseases upon thee." I believe it to be a correct translation.

God did not put the diseases upon Israel. Neither did He put the diseases upon the Egyptians. It is Satan, the god of this world, who has made men sick.

Here Jehovah declares that He is to be Israel's healer.

Exodus 23:25-26, "And ye shall serve Jehovah your God, and he will bless thy bread, and thy water; and I will take sickness away from the midst of thee. There shall none cast her young, nor be barren, in thy land: the number of thy days I will fulfill."

He says He will take sickness from the midst of them. It is a remarkable fact that as long as Israel walked in the Covenant, there was no sickness among them.

There is no record of any babies or young people ever having died as long as they kept the Covenant.

"There shall none cast her young." There were to be no miscarriages nor abnormal abortions.

There were to be no barren wives in the land. Every home was to have children.

"The number of thy days I will fulfill." There were to be no premature deaths. Every person was to grow to full age before he laid down his work.

This is remarkable. Jehovah took over that nation. He became their healer, protector, and supplier of every need.

He was everything they needed.

Deuteronomy 7:13-15, "And he will love thee, and bless thee, and multiply thee; he will also bless the fruit of thy body and the fruit of thy ground, thy grain and thy new wine and thine oil, the increase of thy cattle and the young of thy flock, in the land which he sware unto thy fathers to give thee. Thou shalt be blessed above all peoples: there shall not be male or female barren among you, or among your cattle. And Jehovah will take away from thee all sickness."

Jehovah was to meet every need, supply every demand of that nation.

He was to be intimately in contact with every member of the family.

Everything connected with them was to bear the stamp of prosperity and success. Disease and sickness was not to be tolerated among them.

2 Chronicles 16:11, "And, behold, the acts of Asa, first and last, lo they are written in the book of the kings of Judah and Israel. And in the thirty and ninth year of his reign Asa was diseased in his feet; his disease was exceeding great: yet in his disease he sought not to Jehovah, but to the physicians. And Asa slept with his fathers."

One can see clearly here that Jehovah was displeased with Asa for seeking the help of man when God had promised to be his healer.

Read the Psalms carefully and you will find that God was Israel's healer. It is continually mentioned.

Psalm 103:3, "Who forgiveth all thine iniquities; Who healeth all thy diseases; Who redeemeth thy life from destruction; Who crowneth thee with loving kindness and tender mercies; Who satisfieth thy desire with good things, so that thy youth is renewed like the eagle."

The fact that disease came through disobedience to the Law is evident. Forgiveness for the disobedience meant the healing of their bodies.

* * * * * * * * * * *

We share with Him in His resurrection life.

We reign as kings in the realm of this resurrection life.

You are what He says you are whether you recognize it or not.

You share in all He is or did.

As He was in His earth walk, you are today.

As He is seated at the Father's right hand, you are there legally.

Chapter XVI

PROPHECIES IN REGARD TO THE COMING HEALER

FTER God had told Israel that the reason for disease and sickness was that they had rebelled against the Word of God, condemned the counsel of the Most High, He declared in Psalm 107:17-20:

"Fools because of their transgression, and because of their iniquities, are afflicted." They took themselves out of the protection of the Covenant.

I believe it is in the plan of the Father that no believer should ever be sick, that he should live his full length of time and actually wear out and fall asleep.

It is not the Father's will that we should suffer with cancer, and the other dread diseases that bring pain and anguish.

"Their soul abhorreth all manner of food; And they draw near unto the gates of death. Then they cry unto Jehovah in their trouble, And he saveth them out of their distresses. He sendeth His word, and healeth them, And delivereth them from their destructions."

Men were sick because of broken laws, of sinning against the Word of God. I am speaking now of the Jews.

As they kept the Covenant laws, no illness was among them. But when they sinned, their bodies were filled with diseases. They had a right to turn to the Lord and find their healing.

Practically all the outstanding prophets had the ability to heal the sick under the first Covenant.

Isaiah 53 gives us a picture of the coming Messiah. It is a very graphic description.

3rd verse, "He was despised, and rejected of men; a man of pains and acquainted with disease: and as one from whom men hide their face he was despised; and we esteemed him not. Surely he hath borne our sicknesses and carried our diseases; yet we did esteem him stricken, smitten of God, and afflicted."

This Scripture has to do with the disease problem which confronts the church and the world today, as well as the sin problem.

He has borne our sicknesses, and our diseases. He was stricken, smitten of God and afflicted with our diseases. It was God who laid our diseases on Jesus.

10th verse, "Yet it pleased Jehovah to bruise him; he hath made him sick: when thou shalt make his soul an offering for sin, he shall see his seed, he shall prolong his days, and the pleasure of Jehovah shall prosper in his hand."

God made Him sick with our sickness. He was afflicted with our diseases.

As to our sins, "He was wounded for our transgressions, he was bruised for our iniquities; the chastisement of our peace was upon him; and with his stripes we are healed."

He dealt with man's body, and with his soul, and spirit. He laid our iniquities and our diseases upon Jesus. He was stricken, smitten, and afflicted with our diseases and our sins.

2 Corinthians 5:21, "Him who knew no sin, He made to be sin on our behalf; that we might become the righteousness of God in him."

*   *   *   *   *   *   *   *   *   *   *

He has already healed you.

In the mind of the Father, you are healed.

Jesus knows that He bore your diseases.

How it must hurt Him to hear you talk about bearing them yourself.

Learn to say: "I am healed because He did that work and satisfied the Supreme Court of the Universe."

That makes you free.

Sin shall not lord it over you because you are a New Creation.

When were you healed? When Jesus defeated Satan and stripped him of his authority and arose you were healed.

Chapter XVII

JESUS' MINISTRY

FOLLOWING the temptation, as recorded in Matthew 4:24, He went down out of the mountain and the multitudes thronged Him.

"And the report of him went forth into all Syria: and they brought unto him all that were sick, holden with divers diseases and torments, possessed with demons, and epileptic, and palsied; and he healed them."

In every contact of Jesus with the people, He healed their sick. He did not turn any away. Everyone was healed.

Some would have us believe that there are some cases which are not the will of the Father to heal.

Yet, those same people will take medicine and send for a physician when they declare it is not the will of God to heal them.

The fact is, there aren't any cases that are not the will of the Father to heal. It is not the Father's will that any die of disease.

Sickness does not belong to the body of Christ. It is not normal or natural.

When Jesus said, "I am the vine; ye are the branches," He meant we are united with Him as closely and vitally as the branch is connected to the vine.

You can understand how Jesus could not have cancer, tuberculosis, pneumonia, or any of those other deadly diseases. He is the vine. We, as branches, should have none of these things either.

It is abnormal for believers to be in bondage to poverty so that they have to go to the world for help. Also it is abnormal for them to go to physicians for healing.

The believer is of God. He has been Redeemed out of the hand of the enemy. He has the very nature and life of God in him.

He is the Righteousness of God in Christ. He is not only Redeemed out of the hand of Satan and made a new Creation, but he stands in the Father's presence without the sense of guilt or condemnation.

He has the same liberty and freedom with the Father now that he will have after death when he goes to heaven.

He stands before the Father now as Jesus stood before him.

The Father's love nature has taken the place of the nature of Satan in his life. He is no longer afraid of disease or adverse circumstances.

He is not filled with fear and bondage. The Son has made him free.

Perfect love has cast out fear. He is filled with the nature and life of God, and God's nature is love.

There is no ground for disease and sickness in the body of Christ.

These New Creations are the sons of God, heirs of God, joint-heirs with Jesus Christ.

They have God dwelling in them. They have the life and nature of God, and God, Himself, in the person of the Holy Spirit who raised Jesus from the dead has made His home in their bodies.

Romans 8:11, "But if the Spirit of him that raised up Jesus from the dead dwelleth in you, he that raised up Christ Jesus from the dead shall give life also to your mortal bodies through his Spirit that dwelleth in you."

In the ministry of Jesus there was a perfect coordination between Himself and the Father.

Jesus' attitude toward disease and sin was the Father's attitude.

He lived among the Jews, God's Covenant people, and healed their diseases, breaking Satan's dominion over them individually.

When He went to the cross, He became their Substitute, their Sin-Bearer, their Disease-Bearer.

When He was nailed to that cross, Isaiah 53 became a reality. "Surely he hath borne our sicknesses and carried our diseases; yet we did esteem him stricken, smitten of God, and afflicted."

It was the hand of justice that fell on Him as our substitute as He bore away our diseases.

Chapter XVIII
THE GREAT COMMISSION

THIS is of the most vital importance to every believer. When Jesus was bidding goodbye to the disciples, as recorded in Matthew 28:18-20, He said, "All authority hath been given unto me in heaven and on earth. Go ye therefore, and make disciples of all the nations, baptizing them into the name of the Father and of the Son and of the Holy Spirit: teaching them to observe all things whatsoever I commanded you: and lo, I am with you always, even unto the end of the age."

All authority had been given unto Jesus in heaven and on earth.

He did not need authority. He had always had it. Why was it given to Him now that He was leaving the earth? It was given to Him because He was the head of the church, the first-born from among the dead.

He was the Lord of the Church. The Church was to be His body. He was to use that authority through the Church. All the authority that had been given to Him was for the benefit of the Church.

If there is no way for the Church to use it, then it is ability like our unused capital.

We have, for instance, billions of dollars worth of gold buried in the ground by the government. Some folk think this is a mark of poor judgment, when it could be in circulation bringing blessing to the people.

The Church has done the same thing with the "all authority" that God gave to Jesus. It has buried it in its theology and creeds.

No one seems to have been able to reach it. It is doing no one any good.

The Church does not know that before Jesus went away, He gave to it the power of attorney to use His Name.

This power of attorney gives to the believer access to that "all authority."

"Whatsoever ye shall ask (or demand) in my name, that will I do, that the Father may be glorified in the Son. If ye shall ask anything in my name, that will I do."

This is not prayer. It is the use of the Name of Jesus to draw on this "all authority."

The book of Acts gives case after case where men tapped that "all authority." Men were blessed by it.

That "all authority" is still available to those who use the Name of Jesus. That authority has never been withdrawn.

If one part of that great commission has been abrogated, then all of it has been set aside.

If one miracle has been set aside, then all miracles have been set aside, and the Name of Jesus has no authority. But we know that His Name was given to us for miracle work.

Mark 16: Jesus said, "In my name shall they cast out demons; they shall speak with new tongues; they shall take up serpents, and if they drink any deadly thing, it shall in no wise hurt them; they shall lay hands on the sick, and they shall recover."

Everyone of these five things are things that the adversary brings upon the church of God and the unsaved world.

Five miraculous manifestations are to take place.

Satan holds men in bondage, fills them with fear of poison.

Satan has robbed them of their testimony so they no longer speak in new tongues of deliverance and victory.

They have been robbed of the ability to lay hands on the sick and see their loved ones recover.

Why? Because Sense Knowledge has gained the mastery over the ministry.

Jesus said that as soon as men believed on Him, at once these signs should accompany them. At once they begin to cast out demons. At once they begin to speak with tongues of power. At once they master disease. Serpents are typical of disease and demons.

"So then the Lord Jesus, after he had spoken unto them, was received up into heaven, and sat down at the right hand of God. And they went forth, and preached everywhere, the Lord working with them, and confirming the word by the signs that followed."

The Word that He had spoken, and the Word they dared to confess was confirmed by signs that followed.

God's attitude toward sin and disease has never changed.

Hebrews 13:8, Jesus Christ is the same yesterday, today, and forever. He was opposed to disease then; He is opposed to disease now.

He suffered on account of sin, and His attitude toward sin now is as it was then.

* * * * * * * * * *

The seated Christ is a receipt in full for your healing.
The seated Christ proves that He finished His work.

Always think of Satan as the defeated one, as the one over whom you in Jesus' name have dominion.

In that Name the New Creation is the master of demons and disease and every circumstance that would hold you in bondage.

We have a perfect Redemption, a perfect New Creation, and perfect union with Christ.

"I am the Vine; ye are the branches."

We have a message that brings success, health, happiness, and victory to every man.

Every man is a failure outside of Christ.

We hold God's solution to the human problem.

The Living Word in your lips makes you a victor, makes disease and poverty your servants.

The Living Word in your lips brings God on the scene, brings victory and joy and success to the defeated.

Chapter XIX

GOD'S REVELATION OF JESUS CHRIST GIVEN TO THE APOSTLE PAUL

IN this Revelation we see the supernatural element of Christianity in a light that the modern church has never seen.

Paul's Revelation begins with Jesus being made sin. It deals with what He did, and what was done to Him during the three days and three nights until finally He arose from the dead, carried His blood into the Heavenly Holy of Holies, and sat down at the right hand of the Father.

That period covers the forty days from His crucifixion to His seating at the right hand of the Majesty on High.

It deals with three major facts: What God did for us in Christ in the great Substitution, What the Holy Spirit, through the Word, can do in us in the New Creation, and What Jesus is doing for us now at the right hand of the Father.

We can deal with only two phases of this work of Christ.

What He Did for Us

It is deeply important that the reader fully grasps these basic facts.

Christ did not arise from the dead until He had broken Satan's dominion. It was imperative that Satan's authority over man be broken.

Christ did not arise from the dead until He had conquered the adversary.

Colossians 1:13-14, "Who delivered us out of the authority of darkness, and translated us into the kingdom of the Son of his love; in whom we have our redemption, the remission of our sins."

He delivered us out of Satan's authority. The word here translated "power" means "authority."

He translated us into the kingdom of the Son of His love. That is the New Birth. That is Recreation. We have our Redemption.

Every believer has been delivered out of Satan's authority, and has been translated into the family of God, and has his Redemption in Christ. He is Redeemed. Satan has no more dominion over him.

Romans 6:14 (Centenary translation), "For sin shall not lord it over you."

Sin is Satan. Satan shall not lord it over you. Satan has no more dominion over the believer than Pharaoh had over the children of Israel after they had crossed the Red Sea.

Satan has no dominion over you. Satan cannot put diseases upon you without your consent. It may be a consent of ignorance, but it is a consent.

Satan is defeated, conquered, as far as you are concerned.

Satan is not only conquered, but God has made you a New Creation over whom Satan has no dominion whatsoever.

2 Corinthians 5:17-18, "Wherefore if any man is in Christ, he is a new creation: the old things are passed away; behold, they are become new. But all these things are of God, who reconciled us to himself through Christ, and gave unto us the ministry of reconciliation."

Those old things are the things of defeat, failure, weakness, poverty, sin, and spiritual death.

We are New Creations. Jesus is the head of this New Creation.

He is the Lord of this New Creation. He has taken Satan's place.

Satan no longer has dominion over you. You need have no fear of him, for he has been conquered.

Romans 8:31-38. The Spirit, through the apostle Paul, gives us the position of the Church. He climaxes it in the 38th verse:

"Nay, in all these things we are more than conquerors."

We have a complete and perfect Redemption.

This New Creation has not only been declared Righteous, and been made Righteous, but both God and Jesus declare that they are his Righteousness.

Righteousness means the ability to stand in the Father's presence without a sense of guilt, with the same freedom and liberty that Jesus has.

Why? Because Romans 3:26 declares, "That He might Himself be Righteous, and the Righteousness of him that hath faith in Jesus." (Marginal rendering R. V.)

God has become your Righteousness in Christ Jesus.

1 Corinthians 1:30, God has made Jesus to be Righteousness unto you. This is a most amazing fact.

He does not stop there. 2 Corinthians 5:21, "Him who knew no sin, He made to be sin on our behalf; that we might become the Righteousness of God in Him."

If language means anything, then every believer stands complete in Christ.

Colossians 2:10, "And in him ye are made full (complete), who is the head of all principality and power."

John 1:16, "Of His fulness (or completeness) have we all received, and grace upon grace."

The believer is not a cringing suppliant, begging for favors. He is a son of God, an heir of God, a prince of God.

He stands in the Father's presence, unabashed, unafraid, made Righteous with God's own Righteousness, made free with God's own freedom.

The Son has made you free. You are free in reality. Disease and sickness have no dominion over you.

Had we the space, we could show you that you are not only Redeemed, a New Creation, and the Righteousness of God, but you are a son of God, in His Family.

More than that, the Spirit who raised Jesus from the dead actually makes His home in your body.

You may never have given Him His place, or you may never have been conscious that God made His home in you, or that you had the ability of God in you.

You may have never taken advantage of the fact that your mind might be renewed to the extent that you might know the will of God in reality.

Not only do you have God in you, but you have the Name of Jesus with the Authority that God gave to Jesus in it.

In that Name you can lay hands on yourself if pain comes and receive your deliverance. In that Name you can break the power of the adversary over your finances, over your home, over your loved ones' bodies.

Limitless power and authority are given to the individual member of the Body of Christ.

Some of the Hindrances to Healing

Perhaps the most subtle and dangerous weapons of the devil are the sense of unworthiness, and the sense of lack of faith.

Your worthiness is Jesus Christ, the Righteous. You are the Righteousness of God in Him.

The sense of unworthiness is a denial of the Substitutionary Sacrifice of Christ and of your standing in Christ, and of Christ's Righteousness before the Father which has been granted to you.

A second hindrance is that you have accepted Hope and Mental Assent instead of faith.

You never hope for a thing that you possess. You hope for the unpossessed.

When you hope for your healing, it means that you have no faith in it, but you expect to get it sometime.

Hope is a beautiful delusion. Mental Assent is a kindred of Hope. Mental Assent is the substitute that the adversary has given to the Church today for Faith.

Many declare that the whole Bible is true from Genesis to Revelation, but they do not accept miracles except in isolated cases.

They assent to the truth of the Word, but they do not believe it.

They say, "Yes, I believe the Bible is true," and never act on it.

Believing is acting on the Word of God. There is no Faith without action.

James says in Weymouth's translation that there must be corresponding actions with our faith. "Faith, without actions that correspond, is dead."

There can be no faith without action on the Word. I can assent to it and remain as I am. I can admire it, but it is not mine.

The thing that the Scripture declares belongs to me. As soon as I found out the difference between Mental Assent and Faith, I became a blessing to multitudes.

Many have been healed over the radio when they stopped mentally assenting, and acted on the Word.

Another enemy of Faith is Sense Knowledge evidence. A man believes what he can see. He is like Thomas who said, "I will not believe unless I can put my hand into His side."

Jesus suddenly appeared and said, "Reach hither thy hand, and put it into my side and be not faithless but believing."

Faith is giving substance to things you have hoped for. It is a conviction of the reality of things that are not seen. Faith is changing Hope into reality.

Faith is acting in the face of contrary evidence. The Senses declare, "It cannot be," but Faith shouts above the turmoil, "It is!"

Faith counts the thing done before God has acted. That compels God's action. God is a Faith God.

Hebrews 11:3: The worlds were created by the Word of God so that the things that are seen were not made out of things which do appear.

All God did at the beginning was to say, "Let there be," and there was.

All that Faith has to say is, "Let there be perfect quietness in this man's body and spirit," and disease must go.

Faith says, "Let there be plenty where poverty has reigned. Let there be freedom where bondage has held sway." These things must come to pass.

Chapter XX

HEALING BELONGS TO US

"I HAVE prayed and prayed, and have received no benefit. I have had others pray for me and my disease grows worse and worse. Can you do anything for me?"

"Yes, I believe I can. Did you ever realize that healing belongs to you, that you need not pray for it?"

"I never heard anything like that!"

"It is true. Let me prove it to you.

"Isaiah 53:4, 'Surely he hath borne our sicknesses, and carried our diseases; yet we did esteem him stricken, smitten of God, and afflicted.'

"What does He say He did with our diseases?"

"I don't know as I understand it."

" 'Surely he (that is Christ) hath borne our sicknesses, and carried our diseases; yet we did esteem him stricken, smitten of God and afflicted.'

"You understand that don't you?"

"Yes."

"Do you understand that it pleased Jehovah to bruise Him? He made Him sick with our diseases."

"What does that mean to me?"

"It means that these pains and afflictions you are suffering were laid on Jesus. Jesus actually bore them just as He bore your sins. He was wounded for your transgressions, he was bruised for your iniquities; the chastisement of your peace was upon him; and with his stripes you are healed."

"God actually laid your iniquities upon Jesus. Then you do not have to bear them."

"I never saw it like that before. You mean God actually laid my sickness upon Him, and made Him sick with my diseases?"

"Yes, that is what the Word declares.

"He made Him sin with your sins that you might be the Righteousness of God in Christ; 2 Corinthians 5:21. He made Him sick with your diseases that you might be perfectly well in Christ.

"It is a gift. Healing is yours now, as you thank Him for it.

"God put your diseases on Him. He bore them. He was stricken, smitten of God and afflicted with your diseases. Satan has no right to put on you what God put on Jesus.

"When your heart comes to know this as you know other facts of life, you are through with sickness.

"You cannot be sick when you come to know this fact, know it as you know that God laid upon Him 'the iniquity of us all.'

"Romans 6:14, 'For sin shall not lord it over you' is yours today. I like that translation.

"Sickness and pain are things of the past for 'whom the Son sets free is free in reality.'

"If He has set you free from sin, sin has no dominion over you. If He has set you free from disease, it must not lord it over you. If He has set you free from Satan, Satan has no dominion over you. If He has set you free from circumstances, circumstances cannot lord it over you any longer.

"How they have held sway over us in the past! Now we belong to a new order of things.

"We are the masters of circumstances, of demons, of diseases. Sin and demons have no dominion over us. The Son has set us free.

"In God's sight we are free. In Jesus' sight we are free. According to the Word, we are free.

"Stand fast in the liberty wherewith Christ has made you free. Hold fast to this confession. Make it your very own.

"Take your place. Act the part. Refuse to allow Satan to have anything to do with this body in which you live.

"Know ye not that your body is the temple, the home, the house of God? (I Corinthians 6:15-20.)

"It is God's place. You are the overseer living in it. You are to see that Satan does not trespass on God's property."

"How am I to keep him from it?"

"Jesus said, 'In my name ye shall cast out demons.'

"Jesus has given you the right to use His Name. That Name can break the power of disease, the power of the adversary. That Name can stop disease and failure from reigning over you.

"There is no disease that has ever come to man which this Name cannot destroy."

Our confession is our faith speaking.

Jesus and His Name Are One

That Name and Jesus are one, just as your name is one with you.

You do not have to make this liberty yours. All you have to do is to enjoy it and walk in the light of the Word.

Make these facts your confession. You are to tell the world that by His stripes you are healed, that disease has lost its dominion, that it can no longer lord it over you.

If we speak words of faith instead of words of doubt, we will be speaking God's language. Doubt words come from another source.

You cannot talk sickness and disease, and walk in health.

You cannot tell folk about your disease and about your pains, and moan over your troubles to get sympathy, without losing your fellowship with Him.

When we tell our troubles to people, we lose our faith and sweet fellowship with the Father.

We tell people our troubles to get their sympathy. We should cast our anxiety and troubles upon Him for He cares for us.

When we talk about our weakness and failure and disease, we glorify the devil who gave them to us. We glorify doctors and lawyers by taking our troubles to them. They get paid for listening to people's troubles. That is the secret of their success – being good trouble listeners.

Telling our troubles that are caused by Satan is a confession that Satan is the master and that he has gained the supremacy.

It makes the troubles bigger; it makes the disease worse; it makes us feel worse.

The real confession in our lives should be of God's ability, His faithfulness, and that our troubles are being borne by Jesus just as He bore our diseases and sins.

Hold fast to your confession of what God is to you and what you are in Christ.

Give up your confession of Satan's supremacy. You know that disease comes from the adversary, that lack of ability comes from the adversary. All our troubles are demon-made.

If you are using demon-inspired words, don't expect to have the sweetest fellowship with heaven.

It is the Word of faith which we speak. Our lips are filled with the Word of faith.

Our hearts are singing the song of faith.

John 6:47, "Verily, verily, I say unto you, he that believeth hath eternal life."

It is the believer who possesses. I believe; I have. Then I rejoice in my possession. I enjoy my possession. Health is my possession. Success is my possession.

I have plenty because He is my supply. He meets every need of mine according to His riches in glory in Christ Jesus.

I am not moaning and groaning. I am praising and rejoicing.

Faith possesses. Faith's possessions are real, just as real as Sense possessions.

Spiritual things are as real as material things.

2 Corinthians 5:7, "For we walk by faith, not by sight." We walk in the realm of God. We not only walk by faith, but we talk by faith. We have left the realm of the senses.

When you learn to talk by faith, the dominion of disease is broken over you. But just as long as you walk by reason and you follow the suggestions of the Senses – Feeling, Seeing, Tasting, you are going to live and walk in the realm where disease will hold sway over your life, and pain will hold carnival in your body.

If you will learn to talk faith talk, you will be a victor.

1 John 5:4-5 should be known by every believer. It should be a part of your conscious knowledge that you can use day by day.

"For whatsoever is begotten of God overcometh the world: and this is the victory that hath overcome the world, even our faith."

Some Things That Are Begotten of God

The New Creation is begotten of God. Righteousness is begotten of God. Love is begotten of God. Faith is begotten of God. These are the overcomers of the world.

"Who is he that overcometh the world, but he that believeth that Jesus is the Son of God?" You believe that. That means you are a Victor.

The believers are winners.

Leave the lowlands of doubt and fear. Come out onto the highlands and walk in fellowship with Him.

Healing and victory are yours. Leave failure to the failures.

* * * * * * * * * * *

We are walking with the power of God, fighting with the weapons of Righteousness both for attack and for defense.

"Nay, in all our fight we are more than conquerors."

Why? Because we are raised together with Christ.

When Jesus arose from the dead it was our victory over the enemy.

Conybeare's translation of Colossians 2:15 tells us: "And He disarmed the principalities and powers (which fought against Him) and He put them to open shame, leading them captive in the triumph of Christ."

You remember that we were crucified with Him, died with Him, were buried with Him, suffered with Him, were justified with Him, made alive with Him.

Then we met the enemy and we conquered him in Christ.

So Paul can say to us: "Wherein also ye are made partakers of His Righteousness through your faith in God Who raised Him from the dead."

And God raised Christ so that we might share in His life.

We were made partakers in Christ's resurrection victory, Christ's resurrection life, and Christ's resurrection New Creation.

"Of His fullness have all we received."

"For we are His workmanship created in Christ Jesus."

Chapter XXI

WHAT GOD HATH DECLARED

HERE is the foundation for faith, the Living Word of God. What God says, is. What man says, may be.

What God says is never "may be"; it is always made good. God's Word is a part of Himself, just as your word is a part of you. What you say reveals the real "you."

People come to trust in the "you" in your voice. Your voice and your words are "you."

Jesus was God's voice. What Jesus said, the Father said. Jesus was the Logos, the Word of God. When you read what Jesus said, or you hear it read, you are hearing God, you are hearing the Living Word.

God is back of what He has spoken. The throne of God is back of what He has spoken.

God's character and Jesus' character are involved in what the Father or Jesus has spoken.

So when He says, "Surely He hath borne our sicknesses and carried our diseases, Yet we did esteem Him stricken, smitten of God and afflicted" we know that our diseases were laid on Him.

When He climaxes that statement with, "By His stripes we are healed," we know that we are healed.

It is a problem of the integrity of the Word.

"He was wounded for our transgressions, he was bruised for our iniquities; the chastisement of our peace was upon him; and with his stripes we are healed. All we like sheep have gone astray; we have turned everyone to his own way; and Jehovah hath laid on him the iniquity of us all."

This solves the sin problem.

Hebrews 9:26, "But now once at the end of the ages hath he been manifested to put away sin by the sacrifice of himself."

The sin problem is a settled problem because God said it was settled. Disease and sickness problems are settled because God said that He had settled them.

He bore the diseases.

God said, "By His stripes ye were healed" so that ends the discussion.

He said the issue was closed. The diseases have been put away, so sickness and disease shall not lord it over you.

He said, "Wherefore if any man is in Christ, he is a new creation: the old things are passed away; behold, they are become new."

Disease has no standing with the New Creation. That is His declaration. That statement is a part of Himself.

He says you are a New Creation. He says that you are His son, born from above.

"That which is born of the spirit is spirit." This is a statement of fact.

Sin and disease are one. They cannot dominate the New Creation.

You are not only His son, but you are a joint-heir with Jesus. You are a joint-fellowshipper in all that Christ did and is.

This shows how near you are to Him; "I am the vine, ye are the branches."

God is a part of what He said. In Christ, you are what He says you are.

You are a New Creation created in Christ. "There is therefore now no condemnation to them that are in Christ Jesus" – to the New Creation.

What God says, is. If you are a New Creation, then there is no condemnation for you.

If there is no condemnation, disease cannot lord it over you. If you have committed sins and you confess them, "He is faithful and Righteous to forgive you and cleanse you from all unrighteousness."

You are forgiven. What God says, is. You do not need to make this yours. It was written for you. Just act on it. It is like God. It is a part of God.

If He says He has forgiven you, He has forgiven you. What He has forgiven He forgets. It is as though it had never been.

There is no memory of it. You stand as free as Jesus is in the Father's presence.

Our faulty vision, caused by Sense Knowledge, has made us see as through a glass darkly. The Word has been obscured.

We have not been able to catch God's dream of the reality of it.

The reality of it has never dawned upon the church. They have never realized that they were free from the dominion of Satan.

Colossians 1:13-14, "Who delivered us out of the authority of darkness, and translated us into the kingdom of the Son of his love; in whom we have our redemption, the remission of our sins."

We are delivered out of the authority of Satan. We are translated into the kingdom of the Son of His love.

We are in the kingdom. We are members of it. We are heirs of God and joint-heirs with Jesus Christ.

Satan's dominion is ended. We are free, absolutely delivered. What God says, is. We are Redeemed.

Not only do we have a perfect Redemption, but we have a perfect remission of our sins.

Remission has to do with what we did before we were Born Again.

Forgiveness has to do with what we do after we are Born Again.

Remission is the wiping out of everything connected with our old life.

There are no hangovers in the Divine Life. You are absolutely a New Creation. There are no sin scars upon you.

You are a New Creation created in Christ Jesus. You are the Righteousness of God, created in Christ Jesus.

You are complete in Him. What God has made Righteous is Righteous. What God has declared Righteous is Righteous.

What Jesus made Righteous in His Substitutionary Sacrifice is just what God says it is, a completed, perfect thing in His sight.

When the believer, in the quietness of his own spirit, recognizes the utter integrity of the Word of God, disease, and sickness, and failure are the things of the past.

1 John 4:4, "Ye are of God, my little children, and have overcome them: because greater is he that is in you than he that is in the world."

The power and ability of God is in you right now. You stand a victor in every combat.

You have no apologies to make for weakness. God is the strength of your life.

What God says, is. There is no supposition about it. It is an absolute present-tense reality.

If He says you are more than a conqueror, you are, no matter how mighty the force against you may be.

It makes no difference what Sense Knowledge has told you. You "cast down reasonings" and give the Word of God its place.

You act as though there were not an enemy in the world. When He says, "My God shall supply every need of yours" you are not afraid to do anything He tells you to do.

The money will be there to meet every obligation. God cannot lie. His Word is a part of Himself.

He and His Word are one. He watches over His Word to perform it. He is utterly jealous over His Word. He watches over it with the utmost care.

All you need to do is to call His attention to what He has promised, and He will make the promise good.

God's Word has the ability in it to make good anything He has promised. The Logos of God is a living thing. It produces in the heart of man the very thing He promises He would do.

We preach it and teach it, because it is the living Word today.

God says, "Whosoever believeth in Him shall not be put to shame."

The Living Word

The Word is lifeless until faith is breathed into it on our own lips. Then it becomes a supernatural force.

You may have entire chapters of the Word committed to memory, but they lie dead in your life.

As you act on the Word, it becomes a living thing. Then as you witness, make your confession of that Word, it becomes a dominating force in your lips.

Jesus' Word was the Father's, but He spoke it, He lived it, He acted it. That made it a living thing.

He said, "The words that I speak are not mine, but my Father's words."

"The words that I have spoken unto you are spirit and are life."

We take Jesus' words and we act upon them. That makes them live.

Chapter XXII

WHY I LOST MY HEALING

"I FELT perfectly well for several days after you prayed for me. Then all the symptoms came back and I have been in hell ever since. Can you tell me what is the difficulty?"

"Yes. It is very simple. You received your healing through another's faith. The adversary took advantage of your lack of faith and brought back the symptoms, camouflaged the entire thing and you were filled with fear instead of faith.

"Instead of rising resolutely and meeting the adversary with the Word, and commanding his power broken in Jesus' Name, you yielded.

"Why did you yield? Because you had no foundation in your life. You were like the man who built his house upon the sand. The storm came and destroyed it. The thing for you to do is to get to know the Lord yourself through the Word.

"When you know that 'By His stripes you are healed' and you know it as you know that two and two are four, the adversary will have no power over you.

"When you know the power and authority of the Name of Jesus and that you have a legal right to use it, and the adversary lays siege to you, you will not be filled with fear. You will simply laugh at him and say 'Satan, did you know you were whipped? Leave my body.' He will leave.

"No one can maintain his healing which has come as a result of another's faith unless his faith is developed through the Word, so he can maintain his own rights in the Redemption of Christ."

Chapter XXIII

GOD'S METHOD OF HEALING
IS SPIRITUAL

YOU must have seen as you have studied this book that healing is spiritual.

It is not mental as Christian Science and Unity and other metaphysical teachers claim. Neither is it physical as the medical world teaches. When God heals, He heals through the spirit.

When man heals, he must either do it through the mind that is governed by the physical Senses, or he does it through the physical body.

You understand that man is a spirit being, and that life's greatest forces are spiritual.

We have witnessed a great nation, after months of fearful warfare, conquer one of the smallest nations in the world. They conquered them physically. They are not conquered mentally yet. That will take brutal force. They are not conquered spiritually. They never will be.

We can understand that the great forces in life are spiritual forces.

Love and hate, fear and faith, joy and grief, are all of the spirit.

It is a remarkable thing that when Jesus comes on the scene as a healer, He demands faith. He declares, "Thy faith hath made thee whole." "All things are possible to him that believeth."

We might multiply these statements. All of them prove one thing: that all of Jesus' healings were spiritual. He demanded faith, and faith is born of the spirit.

In our own ministry where we have seen multitudes of people healed of many kinds of incurable diseases they have been healed invariably by the Word of God.

Ps. 107:20, "He sent his word and healed them."

Sin had brought the disease upon them, but the Word delivered them. The Word is the healer today. Man gets his healing by acting upon the Word.

That action is called faith. We have found that healing belongs to the believer.

Chapter XXIV

RIGHT AND WRONG CONFESSIONS

FOR a long time I was confused over the fact that in my own life and the lives of others there was a continual sense of defeat and failure.

I prayed for the sick. I knew that the Bible was true, and I searched diligently to find the leakage.

One day I saw Hebrews 4:14, that we are to hold fast to our *confession*. (Profession in authorized Version.)

In the third chapter of Hebrews, I discovered that Christianity is called "The Great Confession."

I asked myself, "What confession am I to hold fast?"

I am to hold fast to my confession of the absolute integrity of the Bible.

I am to hold fast to the confession of the Redemptive work of Christ.

I am to hold fast to my confession of the New Creation, of receiving the Life and Nature of God.

I am to hold fast to the confession that God is the strength of my life.

I am to hold fast to the confession that "Surely He hath borne my sicknesses and carried my diseases, and that by His stripes I am healed."

I found it very difficult to hold fast to the confession of perfect healing when I had pain in my body.

I made the discovery that I had been making two confessions. I had been confessing the absolute truthfulness of the Word of God, and at the same time I was making a confession that I was not healed.

If you had said, "Do you believe that by His stripes you are healed," I would have said, "Yes, sir, I do."

But in the next breath I would have said, "But the pain is still there." The second confession nullified the first.

In reality I had two confessions: first, a confession of my perfect healing and Redemption in Christ, and a second, that the Redemption and healing was not a fact.

Then came the great battle to gain the mastery over my confession, until I learned to have but one confession.

If I confess that "My God shall supply every need of mine," I must not nullify that confession by saying, "Yes, God supplies my needs, but I cannot pay my rent. I cannot pay the telephone bill."

Faith holds fast to the confession of the Word.

Sense Knowledge holds fast to the confession of physical evidences.

If I accept Physical evidence over against the Word of God, I nullify the Word as far as I am concerned.

But I hold fast to my confession that God's Word is true, that by His stripes I am healed, that My God does supply my needs.

I hold fast to that confession in the face of apparent contradictions, and He is bound to make good.

Many believers have failed when things became difficult because they lost their confession.

While the sun was shining brightly, their confessions were vigorous, strong, and clear.

But when the storms came, the testings came, and the adversary was taking advantage of them, they gave up their testimony.

Every time that you confess disease and weakness and failure, you magnify the adversary above the Father, and you destroy your own confidence in the Word.

You are to hold fast to your confession in the face of apparent defeat.

You are to study the Word until you know what your rights are, and then hold fast to them.

Some make confessions without any foundations. Then the adversary whips and beats them badly.

You are to find out what your rights are. For instance, you know that He says, "Surely He hath borne our sicknesses and carried our diseases." Now you can make your confession.

"Nay, in all these things we are more than conquerors." There you can make your confession.

"Greater is he that is in me, than he that is in the world." You can make your confession here.

Stand by your confession through thick and thin, through good report and evil. You know that your confession is according to the Word.

Revelation 12:11, "And they overcame him because of the blood of the Lamb, and because of the word of their testimony."

Chapter XXV

THE HIGH PRIESTHOOD OF JESUS

ESUS' ministry at the right hand of the Father is one of the rarest features of the Pauline Revelation.

The problem of the authorship of Hebrews is settled. Hebrews is a part of that Revelation.

No one else could have given it as Paul has given it to us. It is a Revelation of what Jesus did from the time He was made sin on the cross, until He sat down on the right hand of the Father.

That entire work is given to us in this wonderful unveiling.

Not only did he make us know what Christ did for us in His Substitution, but he has made us know what the Holy Spirit, through the Word on the ground of the Substitutionary work of Christ does in the individual life.

There are really four phases of this Revelation.

First, what Christ did for us.

Second, what the Holy Spirit, through the Word, does in us.

Third, what Jesus is doing now at the right hand of the Father for us.

Fourth, what His love does through us in ministry.

We spend much time studying what Christ has done for us, but very little time has been given to what He does in us, and less has been given to what He is now doing in His Great High priestly office at the right hand of the Father.

His entire ministries for us would have been a total failure had He not carried on a ministry now at the right hand of the Father on our behalf.

Jesus died as the Lamb. He arose as the Lord High Priest. His first ministry, after He arose from the dead, is illustrated in Jn. 20:15-18.

Jesus met Mary after His Resurrection. She fell down at His feet, and no wonder.

He said to her, "Touch me not; for I am not yet ascended unto the Father: but go unto my brethren, and say to them, I ascend unto my Father and your Father, and my God and your God."

What did He mean? He died as the Substitute Lamb. He arose as the Lord High Priest.

Heb. 2:17, "Wherefore it behooved him in all things to be made like unto his brethren, that he might become a merciful and faithful high priest in things pertaining to God, to make propitiation for the sins of the people."

He is a merciful and faithful high priest, not in things pertaining to man, but in things pertaining to God.

The claims of Justice had to be satisfied as well as the needs of man met.

It was necessary that as a High Priest He should make propitiation for the sins of the people.

This is recorded in Heb. 9:11-12, "But Christ having come a high priest of the good things to come, through the greater and more perfect tabernacle, not made with hands, that is to say, not of this creation, nor yet with the blood of goats and calves, but with his own blood, entered in once for all into the holy place, having obtained Eternal Redemption."

"Christ having come" – from whence did He come? Out of the place where He had gone as a Substitute, when He had met the claims of Justice, where He had satisfied the claims of the Supreme Court of the universe against rebellious humanity.

He had to carry His blood into the heavenly Holy of Holies and seal the document of our Redemption with it.

His blood is the guarantor now of the integrity of our Redemption.

Just as the High Priest under the first covenant carried the blood into the holy of holies once a year and made a yearly atonement, Jesus carried His own blood in and made an Eternal Redemption once for all.

Atonement simply meant to cover the sin of Israel while the sins were borne away by the scape goat.

The sin nature in man that had caused him to break the law (not the act, but the cause of the act), was antagonistic against God and had to be covered.

Now Jesus came and put that Nature away by the sacrifice of Himself.

Heb. 9:26, "But now once at the end of the ages hath he been manifested to put away sin by the sacrifice of himself."

It was not the sins that man had committed; it was man's sin Nature that had to be put away. That sin Nature was spiritual death the Nature of Satan.

His sins were small things that could be wiped out. But that sin Nature required God's own beloved Son to become sin, that we might become the Righteousness of God in Him.

He took our sin that we might become Righteous. He took our spiritual death that we might have Eternal Life.

He took our ostracism, our outlawed nature, that we might take the place of sons with the Father.

Oh the unmeasured grace of God unveiled in the sacrifice of Jesus.

He carried His own blood into the Heavenly Holy of Holies and instead of making the yearly Atonement, He gave us an Eternal Redemption.

Heb. 2:17, "Wherefore it behooved him in all things to be made like unto his brethren, that he might become a merciful and faithful high priest in the things pertaining to God."

He is a merciful and faithful High Priest.

God had to be satisfied. The claims of Justice had to be met.

He was made sin, was under condemnation and for three days and three nights he was in Hell, locked up in the Prison House of Death.

The Supreme Court was able to absolutely Justify Him as our Substitute and declare Him utterly Righteous.

He met the demands of Justice and was liberated.

God said of Him, "This day have I begotten thee."

What day was it He was begotten. It was the third day down in the Prison House of Death that He was Born Again of the Spirit.

That was His New Birth.

That was when we were recreated, for we are His workmanship created in Christ Jesus.

He was there Justified in spirit.

Not only was He declared Righteous, but He was made Righteous with the very nature of God.

Now having been made Righteous, having conquered Satan, stripped him of his authority, He arose from the dead and the Supreme Court of the universe absolutely puts the stamp of approval on His work for us.

Then He was able to go into the heavenly Holy of Holies and sit down at the right hand of the Majesty on High.

He has made propitiation for our sins. That word "Propitiation" means "Substitution."

He has made Substitution for the sins of the people.

Having Himself suffered being tempted, He is able to succor those that are tempted.

Heb. 3:1, "Wherefore, holy brethren, partakers of a heavenly calling, consider the Apostle and High Priest of our Confession."

Christianity is called "a Confession." The finished work of Jesus Christ is called "a Confession."

Now you can understand Rom. 10:9-10, "Because if thou shalt confess with thy mouth Jesus as Lord."

Christianity is a confession.

It is a confession of the finished work of Jesus.

It is a confession that He is seated at the right hand of the Father having perfectly redeemed us.

It is a confession of our sonship, of our place in Christ, of our rights and privileges.

It is a confession of our supremacy over disease and weakness, over Satan in the Name of Jesus.

What a confession that is!

Heb. 4:14-16 carries us a step farther in the development of this High Priestly ministry of Jesus.

"Having then a great high priest, who hath passed through the heavens, Jesus the Son of God, let us hold fast our confession. For we have not a high priest that cannot be touched with the feeling of our infirmities; but one that hath been in all points tempted like as we are, yet without sin. Let us therefore draw near with boldness unto the throne of grace, that we may receive mercy, and may find grace to help us in time of need."

The entire ministry of Jesus swings about this High Priestly office.

As a High Priest, He carried His blood into the Holy of Holies.

As a High Priest He sat down at the right hand of the Majesty on High.

He is the Mediatorial High Priest between God and man.

No man can reach the Father but through Him.

Jesus said, "I am the way, the reality, and the life. No man can get to the Father but by me."

Peter said, Acts 4:12, "And in none other is there salvation: for neither is there any other name under heaven, that is given among men, whereby we must be saved."

Jesus is the only way into the Father's presence without condemnation.

Is it any wonder that the early church was called "The Way."

Acts 9:2, "And asked of him letters to Damascus unto the synagogues, that if he found any that were of 'the Way,' whether men or women, he might bring them bound to Jerusalem."

Acts 19:9, "But when some were hardened and disobedient, speaking evil of 'the Way' before the multitude, he departed from them, and separated the disciples, reasoning daily in the school of Tyrannus."

Acts 19:23, "And about the time there arose no small stir concerning 'the Way'."

Also Acts 24:14&22, Acts 16:17, Is. 30:21, Is. 35:8.

He is not only the Lord High Priest, the Mediator, but the moment a man accepts Christ, He becomes his High Priestly Intercessor.

He ever lives to make intercession for the believer.

Is. 53:12, Rom. 8:34 and Heb. 7:25 He is set forth as the Intercessor for the believer.

He ever lives to make intercession. What a ministry, what a service.

He does not have a chance to take a vacation. He has no opportunity to step aside for a moment.

No one else can act as High Priest, as Mediator, as Intercessor.

He has another important ministry. He is the Advocate.

When the believer is tempted and Satan gains the mastery over him, and he cries out in agony for mercy, we hear Him whisper, (1 Jn. 1:9) "If we confess our sins, he is faithful and righteous to forgive us our sins, and to cleanse us from all unrighteousness."

Then He climaxes it by saying in the next verse, "My little children, these things write I unto you that ye may not sin. And if any man sin, we have an Advocate with the Father, Jesus Christ the righteous." 1 Jn. 2:1.

He is Righteous so that He can go into the Father's presence when we lose the sense of Righteousness by our wrong doings.

As our Advocate, He restores to us our lost sense of Righteousness.

He is the Lord and Head of the Church.

David prophesied of Him in Ps. 23:1, "The Lord is my shepherd, I shall not want."

He is the caretaker, the lover, the bridegroom of the body.

He is the first born from the dead, the head of all principalities and power.

He is my risen Lord seated at the Father's right hand.

Follow me through the entire Epistle of Hebrews and you will find a continual unveiling of these different phases of His High Priestly ministry.

Heb. 4:14, "Having then a great high priest, who hath passed through the heavens, Jesus the Son of God, let us hold fast our confession."

This is the High Priestly Son.

"Let us hold fast our confession." What is our confession? It is our Redemption, our Recreation, our Union with the Father in Christ, our Victory over circumstances and demons and diseases, our Independence in Christ, of natural law.

This High Priest, knowing that man has received an inferiority complex on account of spiritual death says, "Let us therefore draw near with boldness unto the throne of grace, that we may receive mercy, and may find grace to help in time of need."

For we have not a high priest that cannot be touched with the feeling of our infirmities; but one that hath been in all points tempted like as we are, yet without sin."

That word "boldness" means "freedom of speech."

In the Pishito there is a marginal reference which reads, "barefacedness." We are coming without any sense of guilt or sin, as a child would come to an earthly parent.

"For every high priest being taken from among men" has infirmities.

Jesus had no infirmities.

He had nothing but what He took on, from us. He did not come from the seed of Levi. He was not in the priesthood by birth.

He is a priest after an order on the part of God.

Heb. 7:21, "The Lord sware and will not repent himself, Thou art a priest forever; by so much also hath Jesus become the surety of a better covenant."

He is a High Priest, He is the Surety of this New Covenant. The New Covenant heads up in Him.

He was the sacrifice of the Covenant.

His blood was the blood of the Covenant.

His life was the life of the Covenant.

Now He is the Surety of it.

Every scripture from Matthew to Revelation is backed up by the Lord Jesus Himself.

His very throne is back of every Word.

Just as God became the Surety of the Abrahamic Covenant, Jesus now becomes the Surety of this New Covenant.

He can be, because "He abideth forever." He hath His priesthood unchangeable. "Wherefore also he is able to save to the uttermost them that draw near unto God through him, seeing he ever liveth to make intercession for them."

"For such a high priest became us." I think there is no sweeter expression in the entire revelation than this.

Consider Him in all His grace and beauty and His overflowing love.

It is such a High Priest becomes us.

We are New Creations. We are in the beloved.

We are the sweetest, most beautiful things that the Father has.

We are members of His own body.

This Christ says in the 27th verse, "First for his own sins, and then for the sins of the people: for this he did once for all, when he offered up himself."

He was made sin for us.

He made one sacrifice for sins forever, then He sat down at the right hand of the Majesty on High.

Do you realize what it means when it says He sat down?

It means your Redemption is a completed thing.

You are healed.

You are as well as Jesus, in the mind of the Father.

You are an absolute overcomer.

Poverty, want, need, are things of the past.

"That we might receive mercy, and may find grace to help us in time of need."

"My God shall supply every need of yours."

Your heavenly Father knoweth that ye have need of all these things. Jesus demonstrated this in His earth walk.

He fed the multitudes.

He gave the disciples that great draft of fish.

He turned water into wine.

He healed the sick and met every need of man.

That is my Lord.

He is the Mediator of this New Covenant.

He stands between humanity and the Father with the pierced hands and the wounded side and the thorn-scarred brow.

He is the Mediator. Do you think He will turn anyone away who comes to the Father?

Never!

Every unsaved man has a legal right to Eternal Life.

Jesus takes his part and vouches for him the moment he says, "God I will take your Son as my Savior and confess Him as my Lord."

Jesus' High Priestly ministry meets every need of the believer from the moment he is Born Again until he is ushered into the presence of the Father at the end of life.

CONCLUSION

You have read the book.

It will do you no good unless you have made up your mind that you are going to act upon the Scriptures quoted.

The promises that cover your case are of no value until you act upon them.

Believing is acting on the Word.

Faith is the result of action.

But there can be no healing, no deliverance, no victory until you act on the Word.

You may get others to act for you. They will give you temporary relief. What you need is to learn to act for yourself.

It would pay for you to send for our Bible Study course "The Bible in the Light of Our Redemption" and begin to know the Word.

Several people have requested that we include in this book testimonies of the miraculous healings we have seen in our ministry, but we do not consider this wise.

Our purpose in printing this book was that people might see their deliverance in Christ from oppression and sickness, that they might see their complete redemption already purchased for them. We feel that if they were to read of the physical manifestations in others' lives, they would unconsciously look to the other person's healing and not see their own deliverance already accomplished.

For this reason we are leaving this message in the book to be just a statement from the Word of God on our rights and privileges in Christ.

We want you to look to the Word for your healing.